A GUIDE TO TEACHING YOUR CHILDREN HOW TO MASTER MONEY

401 KID

WALTER CLARKE

LEGACY launch pad PUBLISHING

ISBN (ebook): 978-1-964377-64-3

ISBN (paperback): 978-1-964377-60-5

For more information about Walter Clarke and additional resources for 401Kid, scan the QR code below:

CONTENTS

INTRODUCTION

The goal of this book is to serve as both a guide and a wake-up call for parents about the significant consequences of failing to instill financial literacy and entrepreneurial values in their children at an early age. As parents, you have two choices: guide and direct your children toward the endless possibilities of life—or leave them vulnerable to the ever-changing whims of social media and external influences that often act as destructive and corrosive forces on today's youth.

The consequences of inaction are far-reaching and devastating. Many children, lacking a solid foundation of self-worth and direction, fall prey to the darker aspects of modern life. Today's society fosters a culture of comparison and external validation, often amplified by social media platforms where curated, unrealistic portrayals of life leave young people feeling inadequate and unworthy.

Without the tools to understand their value and purpose, children may find themselves trapped in a cycle of depression, isolation and anxiety. They struggle to cope with feelings of insignificance, often retreating into their rooms, avoiding social interaction or developing harmful coping mechanisms. This isolation can lead to a sense of hopelessness, which is a significant contributor to the rising rates of teen suicide.

According to recent statistics, suicide is now one of the leading causes of death among teenagers—a stark reminder of the dangers of neglecting emotional and mental well-being.

Beyond these tragic outcomes, a lack of direction and purpose can result in children falling behind academically and socially. They may disengage from meaningful relationships, hobbies and opportunities that could have been the building blocks of a fulfilling life. In the worst cases, this detachment from reality can spiral into substance abuse as they search for temporary escapes from their pain. Drug rehab centers and mental health facilities are filled with teens who felt unseen, unheard and unsupported during their formative years.

The economic implications are just as dire. Children who are not taught financial literacy or entrepreneurial values often grow up without understanding how to manage money, invest wisely or create opportunities for themselves. This lack of preparation can result in a lifetime of financial struggle—living paycheck to paycheck, drowning in debt and feeling trapped in unfulfilling jobs.

The stakes couldn't be higher. By failing to act, we risk not only the future of our children but also the broader fabric of our society. A generation lacking purpose and resilience contributes to a broader cultural issue of disengagement, entitlement and dependency.

These young people grow into adults who struggle to contribute meaningfully to their communities, perpetuating cycles of poverty, stress and dissatisfaction.

But there is hope—and the power to change lies with us as parents. By teaching core values like financial literacy, entrepreneurship, self-reflection and self-improvement, we can shift our children's focus from external validation to internal confidence. These traits build resilience, grit and a deep understanding of what truly makes us happy. Through these lessons, we can raise confident, empowered individuals who not only thrive themselves but inspire and impact others.

WHAT CAN YOU EXPECT FROM THIS BOOK?

Many people find money principles intimidating, causing their eyes to glaze over when confronted with complex financial concepts. In this book, I simplify the process, breaking down money conversations into manageable building blocks. These discussions will not only impart financial wisdom but also create a priceless, lifelong connection with your child. As a result, get ready to engage in broader and deeper discussions about your child's aspirations and the steps they need to take to achieve them.

As parents, we're no strangers to helping our children build skills and cultivate good habits as they grow. We teach them basic responsibilities like cleaning up after playtime, demonstrating patience and encouraging resilience.

It's time to add financial literacy to that list. This book will empower you to become the financial mentor your child needs to navigate the complex world of money successfully. Who is better positioned to do this than you?

As your trusted guide, I'll provide straightforward and enjoyable ways to discuss money with your child. Each chapter includes valuable life lessons and relatable stories using kid-friendly analogies that make the financial concepts easy to understand (and even fun!).[1]

As you read this book, keep the following in mind:

1. The values you instill in your child will become their compass when they make any life decision.
2. Teach them that challenges are an opportunity to learn and grow.
3. As your child earns money, show them how excess cash provides opportunities.

4. Instead of spending all your money, buy assets.
5. Give to help others.

This book takes readers on a journey to foster these traits in their children and encourages parents to take control of the narrative—regardless of their current financial circumstances—and to do so now. From birth to around 13 or 14 years old, parents have a critical window of opportunity to shape their child's mindset and values. After that, as the saying goes, "the horse is out of the barn" and changing direction becomes significantly harder. The critical question becomes: whose values will shape your child's identity—yours or those of external influences?

Make no mistake: whether you are part of a dual-parent household or a single parent, and regardless of your financial circumstances, you have an obligation to teach your children the entrepreneurial journey. This means understanding the difference between being a wage earner and a business owner who creates impact and fulfillment in their life. The difference between wage income and ownership income is vast, and this distinction must be taught early. You don't have to be a founder to be an owner. Think of the countless millionaires created by companies like Amazon, Walmart and Apple.

There are two paths to walk, and as parents, we must reflect: what do we want for our children?

It's our obligation to show them the possibilities, the barriers and the journey required to achieve success. So much of today's culture is anchored in an outdated narrative: "Get a good job, work a 9-to-5 and retire at 70." But there is so much more to life: self-improvement, self-development and the exhilaration of thinking like an owner. Take this journey with us.

This book focuses on building five key traits in children:

1. **Consistency**
2. **Focus**
3. **Discipline**
4. **Grit**
5. **Resilience**

Entrepreneurship is not just about money. It's about who you become in the process. Just like athletics, it's not about the trophy—it's about the transformation along the way.

Here's the irony: when you teach kids these qualities, they learn how to create value. And when they learn to create value, money follows. With money comes freedom, but everything starts with building these traits.

Build the traits. Build the person. Build the freedom.

KEY TAKEAWAYS

- Start consistent money conversations with your kids early or at the latest, right now.
- Make money conversations fun and turn them into bonding experiences with your kid. Use the "let's learn this together" approach. The earlier you do it the easier it will be. The later you do it, the harder it will be.
- Recognize if you live paycheck to paycheck, you can still learn and teach the principles to your kid by being consistent. I'll be your guide. It all starts with taking that first step. Look no further than Richard Williams for inspiration. He had zero tennis experience and yet he developed his daughters, Serena and Venus, into becoming two of the most talented and celebrated tennis players in the world.
- These money conversations start as tiny habits and should be a consistent part of everyday conversations between you and your child. Over time, they build momentum.
- Utilize the Money Guide at www.401kid.education.

CHAPTER 1

WHEN AND HOW TO TALK TO YOUR KIDS ABOUT MONEY (NOW)

"Life is a game. Money is how we keep score."
—Ted Turner

LESSON: TALK TO YOUR KIDS AS EARLY AS POSSIBLE ABOUT MONEY TO create connection points and meaningful bonds with them that will last a lifetime.

I was blown away by the TED Talk, *How Any Child Can Thrive By Five*, with over 12 million views. The speaker is seven-year-old Molly Wright, one of the youngest-ever TED speakers. She asks, "What if I was to tell you that a game of peek-a-boo could change the world?" And then she dives into the importance of parents engaging with their kids using the example of one-year-old Ari and his dad.

Wright goes on to show how the first five years of a child's life is the most important stage of their development as that is when their learning/adapting capabilities peak. Wright seeks to raise awareness about the importance of brain development in the early years of a child's life, as well as the impact it has on their future.

She highlights the benefits of play on lifelong learning, behavior and well-being, sharing effective strategies to help all kids thrive by the age of five. What she is advocating is what this book is all about. Parents, put your devices down and pay extra attention to your kids, especially during these crucial first five years of learning.

As Wright points out, as a parent, you are in a unique position. When your kids are young, they are pliable—and all they want to do is be around their parents. In their eyes, you are the coolest. You are practically Superman. Just like you want to model good behavior to your kids, the same kind of consistency applies to these money conversations.

Even if you have teenagers and believe you missed your opportunity, you haven't. Consistency is the key. It's like going to the gym. If you go to the gym four times over the course of a couple of months, you're not going to see many results. However, if you go five times a week and subscribe to a workout program for a year, you *will* see results. The same principle applies to money conversations: to make real change you need to be consistent.

WHY DON'T PARENTS WANT TO TALK TO THEIR KIDS ABOUT MONEY?

Parents shy away from discussing finances with their children for a variety of reasons. Some don't see the relevance, questioning the need to talk about money with kids who don't have any. Others find financial concepts too complex for little kids, often struggling with them themselves, which perpetuates a cycle of uncertainty. There's also a fear that teaching children about money might make them feel entitled.

This reluctance mirrors the misguided belief that avoiding discussions about drugs or sex will prevent your kids from thinking about it. In reality, such avoidance often leads to a lack of understanding and preparedness.

Teaching kids about money can be challenging for parents, as it often requires them to examine and improve their own financial literacy. While this can be uncomfortable, it's ultimately empowering for both parents and children as they work together to create a healthier relationship with finances.

Financial education from an early age is crucial. Parents, as primary educators about financial discussions, often fall into four categories:

- **Financially Struggling Parents:** May avoid money talks due to embarrassment or stress about their situation.
- **Financially Stable Parents:** Might overlook teaching money management, assuming financial security is a given.
- **Wealthy Parents:** May delay financial discussions, believing their wealth will naturally educate their children.
- **Multigenerational Wealth Parents:** May avoid money talks to protect children from wealth's burden or assuming family assets will suffice.

Each of these four types of parents has their reasons for avoiding these crucial conversations, whether it's discomfort, perceived inadequacy, or a belief that it's unnecessary. Addressing these barriers is key to fostering financial literacy and creating more financially savvy future generations. Early and open discussions about money are invaluable during this time, and I cannot emphasize enough the importance of having these money conversations early.

WILL THESE CONVERSATIONS *REALLY* MAKE A DIFFERENCE TO YOUNG KIDS?

Yes. It all goes back to early childhood development research. Scientists refer to a phase when children's brains rapidly evolve as a "critical period." During this timeframe, children can learn and grasp new languages better. As this window closes, it gradually becomes harder for people to reach fluency in a new language.

This "critical period" is also relevant when teaching your kids about money too. Kids are smart and have a perpetual curiosity, which is great for learning new things at a young age. To put this in perspective, think about the eating habits you formed early on and how that has influenced your taste buds today.

When I had guests visiting from Australia, as a good host, I asked if they had any special requests. They wanted Vegemite, a staple food for Australians. It's a black paste that I think is the nastiest food ever, but if you grew up in Australia, it's like candy. That's because Australians introduce Vegemite into their infant's diet right from the start.

If you feed your kids sugary donuts and other processed food at a young age, convincing them to eat healthy later on is extremely difficult as they have already built a foundation of choosing food for comfort rather than nutrition. In contrast, one of my friends introduced broccoli to his kid when he was an infant. Today, his kid can't get enough of it. If you wait to introduce broccoli to your kids after the age of six, the chances of them liking broccoli goes down exponentially, but if you raise them on it, they'll grow to love it. I'm convinced that we can spoon feed our kids money conversations at a young age just like broccoli or Vegemite. By doing so, it will influence the way they view and handle money for the rest of their lives.

It is foundational to instill the idea of saving, spending, investing and giving away money early. This approach fosters discipline and an understanding that you can't spend every nickel that comes your way. You need to give some of it away to those less fortunate, save for a rainy day, and invest in your future to achieve financial stability later in life.

It's akin to choosing between Vegemite or broccoli versus indulging in donuts—children often grow up spending every nickel they receive. Consequently, transitioning from being a big spender to a big saver becomes much harder as they grow older. These conversations are easier when they're young; later on, the shift becomes increasingly challenging. The initial discussions pave the way for healthier financial habits in the future.

The importance of having conversations early on with children lies in their natural curiosity and openness. At a young age, kids are neutral about many things because they haven't yet formed strong opinions yet. They're just curious about life. Introducing these discussions early allows children to be more adaptable and receptive, creating a solid foundation in a neutral environment. This foundation becomes ingrained in their DNA, contrasting with opinions shaped by external influences as they grow older.

For instance, when you introduce concepts to a three or four-year-old, they're very open and willing to learn, without biases or strong opinions. However, with a 12-to-14-year-old, you're likely to encounter strong opinions and potential conflicts with their existing worldview. At this stage, gaining traction in conversations can be challenging, and they might even view your ideas as foolish. Starting these discussions early helps in building a more adaptable and open mindset in children.

If you haven't had a discussion with your kids about money, ask yourself *why*.

SO, HOW CAN YOU NATURALLY INTRODUCE THE TOPIC OF MONEY WITH KIDS?

Money is a part of our everyday lives and an easy topic to bring up regardless of your child's age. Start simple and stay consistent. Those money conversations will start by exploring:

- What money is and how it works
- What earning money looks like

- How doing tasks leads to rewards (like something as simple as a sticker)
- How money is a measurement
- How money encompasses saving, spending, investing and giving it away

Consider developing a game or maintaining a consistent conversation each time your child receives money—or even when you do. Introduce the concept of the dollar by discussing how they can spend, save, invest and give away. Explain that saving is for a rainy day or emergencies, investing is like planting a garden that grows over time, and giving helps those less fortunate and puts back into the stream of life.

The topics of spending, saving, investing and giving away money can lead to profound and valuable conversations with your toddler. Speak to them as if they understand, and over time, you'll be surprised at how quickly they do. It's possible to instill financial discipline in a four-year-old, teaching them the importance of restraint and thoughtful spending!

To broach the topic of money with your young child, share the following story:

It was a sunny afternoon, and Lily was playing with her five favorite dolls that each have unique personalities, especially when it comes to money.

Penny the Saver is always clutching her piggy bank. She'd say, "Every coin counts! Let's save for a rainy day." Penny felt safest when she had money tucked away, and she never spent without careful thought.

Sammy the Spender's pockets were always empty because he loved buying new toys. "Life's too short! Let's have fun now," he'd shout. Sammy believed money was meant to be enjoyed at the moment.

Gina the Giver believes "Sharing is caring! How can we help others?" Gina found joy in using her money to make others happy and support good causes.

Eddie the Earner is always busy working at various jobs. "Hard work pays off! What can I do to earn more?" he'd say. Eddie knew that making money took effort, but he enjoyed the challenge.

Izzy the Investor is always thinking about the future. "Let's make our money grow!" she'd suggest. Izzy loved the idea of turning a little money into more over time.

Lily decided the dolls should have a playdate at the park. As they "walked" there, they passed a toy store.

Sammy the Spender got excited and said, "Oh! Let's buy that new ball in the window!"

Penny the Saver shook her head. "But we already have balls at home. We should save our money."

Gina the Giver had another idea. "What if we buy the ball and donate it to kids who don't have any toys?"

Eddie the Earner chimed in, "Or we could do some chores to earn money for the ball."

Izzy the Investor suggested, "Let's invest in a company and watch it grow."

Lily smiled, realizing that each doll had a different, important way of thinking about money. She knew that in real life, it was good to be a little bit like each doll—saving some, spending wisely, giving to others, earning through hard work and investing for the future.

As she played in the park, Lily imagined all five dolls working together, combining their money skills to make the best decisions. She knew that one day, she'd be able to do the same.

Sharing stories like these are a natural segue into how they can do tasks and receive rewards. At this young age, money conversations are more about showing the connection between effort and outcomes, not about the actual money itself. You can begin by using things like tokens or stickers as rewards for tasks. The more our kids have these types of experiences, the stickier these ideas will be.

Age-appropriate tasks for a three-year-old might include picking up toys or putting dirty clothes in a laundry basket. You could give them a sticker or token each time they do these activities to reinforce the task-reward system. After accumulating a certain amount of stickers or tokens, they can trade them in for a reward like extra playtime or a special treat. This is the perfect time to talk about money. I wrote a book called, *The Adventures of the Magic Penny*, to teach young kids about money lessons. Buy my children's book series at www.401kid.education.

WHAT ARE SOME OTHER WAYS TO SHOW HOW TASKS LEAD TO REWARDS?

The opportunities for showing how tasks lead to rewards are truly endless. You can kickstart your child's money journey by getting a savings and investment app like Robinhood, GoHenry or Greenlight. Robinhood requires you to be at least 18 years old to invest. However, you can use their allowance or other money they make doing chores to deposit the money and watch their money grow. Do a careful Google search and read the fine print to see which app might work best for you and your family. The end goal should be having your kid learn the value of saving money today so they can invest in their future.

You might explain saving money on the app in this way to a younger child:

A savings account is a grown-up digital version of a piggy bank and I want you to have one. And I'm going to help you grow your money faster by playing something with you called Match Game.

Chances are, if you bring up the idea of another game, it will pique their interest. After all, most kids can relate to playing games. Together, open the savings account so they feel vested in the end result.

The Match Game is a simple way to get your child interested in saving money so they can invest it later. As they begin earning money doing age-appropriate chores, you tell them you will match each dollar they place in their savings account. Kids can grasp the concept of two-for-one pretty easily. You incentivize your children to save money because it is a game where they will emerge the winner every time. On a regular basis, you will review the account balance together so they can see how their money is growing.

Eventually, as they see the rewards of playing the Match Game, you can start having conversations about investing. Explain how savings accounts invest in their future financial well-being. As their parent, you will play an important role here, as young kids naturally want to emulate and copy their parents.

There are all kinds of financial literacy games that teach kids of all ages about saving and investing in fun interactive ways.[1] Be sure to work together to find and play these types of games with your child. Money conversations flow easily as your child begins to grasp the value of money. Not only are they learning about simple money concepts, but they are also using basic math skills. That's important because as we learn, we increase our ability to earn money.

You owe it to your kids to have these money conversations early and often. It doesn't matter whether you are ultra-wealthy, living paycheck-to-paycheck or somewhere in between. All kids should have an equal opportunity to learn about money whether their parents have a little or a lot of money. The powerful lessons they learn today will prove invaluable tomorrow.

By having these money conversations with your child, you'll influence their perception of and relationship with money for the rest of their lives. It's never too early to instill good financial habits. By engaging your child in these conversations early, you'll be providing them a solid foundation for their future financial success.

Remember that learning new things, whether walking, talking or riding a bike is a process. Money is no exception. You don't need to be perfect. The key is to simply start. You won't be perfect, and you'll make mistakes along the way, but engaging in the conversation will lead to the right path and be a tremendous learning experience. It's similar to an overweight person going to the gym for the first time. They may feel intimidated and know they need to go, but starting is the hardest part. Overcoming that initial discomfort is crucial. There's also a tremendous sense of satisfaction when you conquer that challenge.

The same goes for learning about money. I've had students come to me saying, "I just can't learn this." But once they engage in the conversation and participate in the dialogue over time, they come back and say, "Oh my God, this isn't that difficult. Why was I so reluctant to start? I'm so grateful I did." Just like the overweight person in the gym, the important thing is to start, be easy on yourself and strive for consistency. And when you stumble, just laugh and keep going.

KEY TAKEAWAYS

- You owe it to your kids to have these money conversations as soon as possible.
- The sooner these conversations begin, the more ingrained they become in your child's life.
- Have the conversations before they have the urge to hear them.
- Complete the Start it Now Worksheet at www.401kid.education as it's key to a strong financial foundation.
- Read *The Adventures of the Magic Penny* with your child.
- Read more stories at www.magicpenny.education.

CHAPTER 2
TEACH CORE VALUES TO YOUR KIDS EARLY

"Whatever things you go through, you stay true to who you are and your core values."
—Sophie Gregoire Trudeau

LESSON: CONSIDER CORE VALUES TO BE THE BUILDING BLOCKS OF who you are and how you act. When kids learn how important these values are early on, they grow up with a solid idea of right and wrong. This helps them make good choices based on what really matters, not just what's easy or quick. If you don't inform your child's core values, the internet will.

While walking along the beach one morning on vacation, I encountered a family where the kids were all sitting in beach chairs in a circle. The three boys and one girl ranging in ages 10-16 were reading intently and appeared to be enjoying it. I don't encounter this type of thing very often so I struck up a conversation with their father. He explained that the kids were reading books on the beach because of the core values he taught them. He shared:

- We talked about sex before they had desires.
- We talked about dating before they wanted to date.

- We talked about money before they had money.
- We talked about social media before they wanted phones.
- We talked about service to others before they understood time.

He told me his goal was to have many uncomfortable conversations with his kids early on. While these conversations were hard, they were manageable because the kids eventually understood the value of them and what their dad was trying to do. One of the most important conversations he had was about money before the kids had any money.

WHAT CAN WE LEARN FROM THIS FAMILY ON THE BEACH?

Early on, the father instilled a strong foundation of core values in his children. These core values became essential as they navigated the myriad challenges of growing up, one of the most significant of these being money. In a world filled with conflicting messages about wealth, status and materialism, having a clear set of values provided them with a guiding light.

As children mature, they encounter various situations that test their values. Friends might flaunt their latest gadgets, or social media might promote a lifestyle centered around consumerism. In these moments, the father's teachings became a crucial reference point. He would remind his kids of the values they had discussed—honesty, hard work and the importance of saving for the future. This consistent reinforcement helped the children stay anchored to their moral compass, even when external pressures tempted them to stray.

Without this strong foundation, discussions about money and its implications could have been much more difficult. The complexities of financial decisions often come with emotional weight, and navigating them without a clear understanding of your core values can lead to confusion and poor choices. The father's proactive approach made these conversations more manageable. Although they were still challenging, the framework of values provided a context within which they could understand the implications of their choices.

Over time, the children gradually came to appreciate and internalize these lessons. They not only understood the significance of money but also recognized the importance of aligning their financial decisions with their core beliefs. They became more mindful of their spending habits and learned to differentiate between needs and wants. This awareness allowed them to evaluate outside influences critically, helping them see trends and advertisements for what they truly were—temporary distractions rather than long-term goals.

This journey wasn't without its difficulties. The process of learning to prioritize values over immediate gratification involved struggle and conflict. However, these experiences ultimately strengthened the family unit. They developed open lines of communication where money and values could be discussed without fear of judgment. This atmosphere of honesty encouraged the children to express their concerns and questions about financial matters, leading to deeper understanding and respect for their father's guidance.

This exercise has proven invaluable for this family. Grounded in their beliefs and values, these children have forged a resilient identity that equips them to face financial challenges with confidence. They've learned not just to react impulsively to external pressures but to pause, reflect and make decisions that align with their principles. This holistic approach to financial education—rooted in core values—has empowered them to navigate the complexities of adulthood while maintaining their integrity and sense of self.

When you think about it, it makes perfect sense. We speak to our kids the moment they are born, but they don't understand what we are saying or talk back. That doesn't stop us from talking to them. It simply comes naturally. The same philosophy should apply to having money conversations: early and often. Bring them into the conversation about money in every way possible before they understand what money is. Soon, it will become part of their DNA and they become hard-wired to have these money conversations as they grow up.

These conversations are a bonding opportunity and create the kind of connection many parents are lacking with their kids. Money conversations are just an avenue to creating unity and connection with your kid. The indirect benefit is elevating their financial literacy. They're going to be more aware of their financial acumen because you are communicating these concepts consistently and early on.

In today's rapidly evolving world, where technology and social dynamics constantly shift, it is more crucial than ever to instill core values in our kids. These core values act as a bedrock for behavior, guiding kids through the complexities of growing up and helping them navigate the moral and ethical challenges they will inevitably face. Establishing a strong value system early on not only shapes character but also influences decision-making, resilience and the ability to form meaningful relationships. As a parent, you want to be the one to instill these values.

WHAT CAN HAPPEN WHEN YOU DON'T INSTILL THOSE STRONG CORE VALUES?

When people have weak values, they become easily influenced by the pressures of trying to fit in and impress their peers. Consider situations like the first time someone is offered drugs, cigarettes, vape or is pressured into sexual activity. If that person lacks a solid foundation in their beliefs and a clear understanding of who they are, they are more likely to succumb to these kinds of pressures.

When you're not grounded, the allure of being accepted and perceived as cool can overshadow your inner sense of right and wrong. This often leads to choices that contradict your true values because the immediate reward of social acceptance seems more appealing than the long-term consequences of violating your core values.

Children and teenagers who haven't yet developed strong values are more susceptible to the influence of others, often prioritizing the need to belong over their personal beliefs. Without a strong value system, they can easily be led astray by peer pressure, making decisions that can have detrimental effects on their lives.

Having strong values acts as a guiding compass, helping people make decisions that align with their true selves, even in the face of external pressures. It enables them to stand firm in their beliefs and resist the temptation to engage in behaviors that go against their principles.

HOW CAN CORE VALUES HELP WITH HAVING MONEY CONVERSATIONS WITH KIDS?

Core values such as honesty, respect, responsibility and empathy are the pillars upon which character and integrity are built. When children learn the importance of these values from a young age, they develop a sense of self that is rooted in principles rather than convenience or expediency. This intrinsic understanding of right and wrong fosters integrity, ensuring that kids grow into adults who act consistently with their beliefs and are trustworthy in their personal and professional lives.

Here's how these core principles can influence how your kids view money or life. In today's fast-paced and ever-evolving world, the importance of instilling core money values in youth cannot be overstated. Financial literacy and responsible money management are essential skills that can significantly impact our future success and well-being. The values and attitudes that young people develop toward money will shape their financial behaviors and decisions throughout their lives.

Financial literacy is built on core money values, which serve as guiding principles for financial behavior. These values include responsibility, discipline, patience and a sense of security. By instilling these values in young people, we provide them with a framework for making sound financial decisions and developing healthy financial habits.

WHAT ARE SOME BENEFITS OF KIDS LEARNING FINANCIAL LITERACY AT A YOUNG AGE?

Empowerment and Confidence: When young people understand financial concepts and feel confident in their ability to manage money, they are empowered to take control of their financial future. This confidence can lead to more proactive financial behaviors, such as saving for long-term goals and avoiding unnecessary debt.

Better Decision-Making: Financial literacy enables the youth to make informed decisions about spending, saving and investing. With a solid understanding of financial principles, they can evaluate options more critically and choose those that align with their long-term goals.

Reduced Financial Stress: Money is a common source of stress for many people. By teaching young people how to manage their finances effectively, we can help reduce this stress and promote overall well-being. Financially literate people are better equipped to handle unexpected expenses and financial challenges without experiencing unnecessary anxiety.

Long-Term Financial Stability: Developing good financial habits early in life sets the stage for long-term financial stability. Youth who understand the importance of saving, investing, and living within their means are more likely to achieve financial security and independence as adults.

Preparation for Future Responsibilities: As young people transition into adulthood, they will face a variety of financial responsibilities, such as paying for education, housing, and healthcare. Financial literacy prepares them to handle these responsibilities effectively and avoid common pitfalls, such as excessive debt and poor credit management.

Core values form the foundation for the structure of our lives. They create a compass by which we measure ourselves. The stronger the bedrock, the deeper the values, and the stronger the house, the structure of our lives, will be. In an environment of turbulence and disturbance, the world will always throw events and opportunities at us that tempt us to deviate from our mission and values.

This compass becomes our guide while our deeply rooted values help create what is probably the single most important characteristic for ensuring our success: self-discipline. Self-discipline is the ability to do the right thing even when everything outside tells you to do something else. It helps us resist the temptations and distractions that conflict with who we are at our core.

The Secret Race, a book about doping in the Tour de France, shows how cyclists violated their ethical compasses. They did so both because everybody else was doing it, and also because there was a greater goal that seemed to justify violating this core value. I think we all face similar situations at some point in our lives, and I am by no means suggesting that I would have done anything different. We continually face these particular issues. The point is that the stronger our bedrock is, the more likely we are to adhere to our core principles and values. If the foundation is weak, it is more likely that the world will affect us, and that we will regret decisions we made that compromised our values, particularly with our money.

WHAT DOES FINANCIAL FREEDOM LOOK LIKE IN REAL LIFE?

Financial freedom means having enough money to do the things you need and want to do without worrying about running out. It's having a bank account that always has plenty of money in it, allowing you to buy things you like, save for the future and help others in need. With financial freedom, you can make choices that bring you happiness and security without being stressed about money. Money is just a tool on the path to achieving life balance. Your kids will be fiscally responsible and disciplined so as money comes to them, they will intuitively know how to utilize it.

The following is an example of what financial freedom can be when you pay attention to your core values. Once upon a time, there was a young man named Jordan who grew up in a modest home with his single mother, Lisa. She worked as an accountant and believed that the best gift she could give her son was not material wealth, but the knowledge and discipline to manage money wisely.

From the time Jordan was six, Lisa began teaching him the basics of money. She made it fun by giving him three jars labeled Spend, Save and Give. Every time Jordan received an allowance or birthday money, they would sit down together and talk about how to divide it up. A portion always went into the Spend jar for small treats, another into the Save jar for bigger dreams, and the last portion into the Give jar to donate to causes Jordan cared about.

As Jordan grew older, the lessons evolved. By the time he was ten, Lisa introduced him to the concept of investing. She explained stocks, real estate and how businesses made money.

Together, they opened a small brokerage account for him, where he could track a few stocks that piqued his interest. "It's not about the money," Lisa would say, "it's about understanding how the world works and making your money work for you."

Jordan's interest in finance grew. At 16, he saved up enough from part-time jobs and investing small amounts of money that his mom helped him invest in a low-cost index fund. She explained how companies grew over time and how patient, consistent investing could be his key to finding financial freedom.

One summer, when Jordan turned 21, his life took an unexpected turn. His late grandfather, whom he barely knew, had left him a substantial inheritance. When the lawyer read the will, Jordan found himself the beneficiary of nearly half a million dollars. His friends were awestruck—some even jealous—but Jordan didn't panic or rush out to buy luxury items. Thanks to his mother's lessons, he understood the importance of this windfall and knew what to do next.

The first thing he did was sit down with his mother to develop a plan. Together, they outlined clear goals: paying off any educational debt, putting aside a portion for a future home and investing the rest in a diversified portfolio of stocks and real estate. Instead of blowing through the money, Jordan decided to continue living a modest life, letting his investments grow while he pursued his own passions in life, which included starting a small business.

Through his journey, Jordan realized that it wasn't the sudden wealth that made the difference. It was the early education from his mother that empowered him to handle it wisely. He stayed focused, used the money to enhance his opportunities and ensured that it would last for generations to come.

Years later, Jordan paid it forward. Just like his mother had done with him, he started teaching financial literacy to kids in his community, always reminding them that money is a tool and the true wealth lies in understanding how to use it wisely.

IN WHAT OTHER WAYS CAN THESE CORE VALUES HELP US?

Guide Decision-Making: Kids equipped with strong core values possess a moral compass that guides their decision-making processes. In situations where peer pressure, societal expectations or momentary desires might lead others astray, these kids rely on their ingrained principles to choose paths that align with their values. This not only helps them avoid negative influences and risky behaviors but also empowers them to make choices that promote their well-being and the well-being of those around them.

Enhance Emotional Resilience: Teaching core values like perseverance, courage, and kindness helps build emotional resilience. Life is filled with challenges, failures and setbacks. Young people who understand the importance of perseverance are better equipped to face adversity with a positive attitude. Values like courage help them stand up for what is right even in the face of opposition, while kindness fosters empathy and compassion, creating a supportive and nurturing environment that enhances emotional well-being.

Foster Strong Relationships: Relationships are the cornerstone of a fulfilling life, and core values play a vital role in developing and maintaining these connections. Respect and empathy enable young people to understand and appreciate the perspectives of others, promoting healthy communication and reducing conflicts. Responsibility and fairness ensure that they contribute positively to their relationships, whether with family, friends or colleagues, fostering mutual trust and cooperation.

Integrate Values into Daily Life: Incorporating core values into daily routines and interactions helps reinforce their importance. Simple acts such as sharing, helping others, expressing gratitude and acknowledging efforts can make these values tangible for children. Parents and educators should seize teachable moments to discuss the significance of these actions and the values they represent, creating a continuous learning environment.

Provide Opportunities for Practice: Children learn best through experience. Providing opportunities for them to practice core values in real-life situations solidifies their understanding and application. Group activities, community service projects and collaborative tasks in school and at home can help children see the positive impact of values like teamwork, generosity, and responsibility.

Shape Future Leaders: The youth of today are the leaders of tomorrow. By instilling core values early in life, we are nurturing a generation who will lead with integrity, compassion and a strong sense of justice. These future leaders will be equipped to address societal challenges, promote ethical practices and inspire others to uphold these values as well, creating a much more just and compassionate world.

Promote Social Harmony: A society built on shared core values is more cohesive and harmonious. When young people grow up with a strong sense of respect, empathy and responsibility, they contribute to a community where people support each other and work together towards common goals. This collective adherence to positive values reduces conflicts and fosters a sense of belonging and unity.

Ensure Personal Fulfillment: Ultimately, living according to core values leads to personal fulfillment. People who align their actions with their principles experience a sense of purpose and contentment. They build meaningful relationships, achieve personal and professional goals with integrity, and contribute positively to society. This sense of fulfillment is a crucial aspect of a happy and successful life.

WHAT'S THE BEST WAY TO SHOW YOUR KIDS CORE VALUES?

Parents and educators are the primary role models for children. Demonstrating core values through behavior is far more impactful than merely discussing them. When adults consistently exhibit integrity, respect, and empathy, children observe and internalize these behaviors. Through this children understand that these values are not just abstract concepts but practical and vital aspects of everyday life.

Teaching core values to today's youth is an investment in the future. By establishing a bedrock of behavior rooted in principles such as honesty, respect, responsibility and empathy, we are shaping kids who can navigate the complexities of life with integrity and resilience. Parents and educators play a pivotal role in this process, modeling these values and providing opportunities for children to practice and internalize them. The long-term impact is profound, influencing not only the personal success and fulfillment of their kids but also the collective well-being and harmony of society.

As we guide our kids in their formative years, remember that the values we impart today will shape the leaders, citizens and compassionate human beings of tomorrow. As your child's parent, you are their most important mentor.

What does this have to do with building wealth? Everything. The better your kids' moral compass, the better they will be at managing life's inevitable challenges. What makes money conversations tough is when kids are taught that outside pleasures are more important than their morals and values.

Because we live in a world where material possessions are highly valued, the Smiths made a conscious decision to prioritize their kids' moral compass early on. Knowing life's inevitable challenges, they wanted to instill solid core values in their kids so they could better navigate life's twists and turns.

Through daily conversations, volunteer work and leading by example, the Smiths instilled values of honesty, empathy and perseverance in their children. As their children grew, they faced challenges with remarkable resilience, a testament to their strong character that set them apart from their peers.

However, the real test came when the family moved to a more affluent neighborhood. Suddenly, their kids were surrounded by classmates who measured their worth by the latest gadgets and designer labels. The pressure to fit in was immense, and money conversations at home became increasingly difficult.

The Smiths constantly reinforced the idea that true fulfillment comes from within, not from external possessions. It was an uphill battle against the tide of consumerism, but they persevered, knowing that by staying true to their values, their children would be better equipped to face not just financial challenges but any obstacle life might throw their way. The perseverance paid off. The kids used their strong core values to navigate the situation. Their parents anchored the core values early on in their kids, which naturally shaped their foundation for future behavior.

KEY TAKEAWAYS

- Remember that teaching core values to your kids is a long-term investment.
- Core values provide the foundation for developing practical money management skills and healthy financial habits that will last a lifetime.
- Complete the core values worksheet at www.401kid.education.

CHAPTER 3
THE VALUE OF THE LEARNING JOURNEY

"It's supposed to be hard. If it wasn't hard, everyone would do it. The hard...is what makes it great."
–Jimmy Dugan, *A League of Their Own*

LESSON: LEARNING IS THE GATEWAY TO FREEDOM AS IT OPENS OUR kid's eyes to a world full of possibilities. While the journey may be challenging, it lays the foundation for achieving the ultimate goal: creating meaningful value in the world.

Learning expands everything we do and provides greater choices and opportunities down the line. Consider a baby who is just learning how to crawl. Watch the elation on their face as they experience the freedom of being able to crawl. Their world expands exponentially. And then think about how learning to walk provides such incredible freedom.

Or, think about learning to drive and getting the keys to your first car—how much freedom does that give you? The list goes on and on as we eventually move out of our parent's home, go to school and get our first job.

Imagine if we never bothered to take that first step—to venture out and expand our horizons because we were complacent? So many opportunities are lost. That's why I'm a huge advocate of continuing education and acknowledging the value of learning new things.

When we work hard and dedicate time to developing our skills, there is often a direct correlation between how proficient we become and the amount of value we can create. This value could be measured through the quality of our work, the impact we have on others or the tangible outcomes we achieve in our professional or personal lives. However, no matter how skilled we become, there is always room for growth and improvement. By continuously learning and enhancing our skill set, we can increase our potential to create even greater value. This ongoing process of self-improvement not only makes us more effective in our chosen fields but also helps us adapt to new challenges and opportunities as they arise. The pursuit of excellence is a lifelong journey, where each step forward opens up new possibilities for learning and growth.

COULD YOU SHARE MORE ABOUT THE LEARNING JOURNEY AND CREATING VALUE?

As a landscaper, when you mow someone's lawn, you are creating value. Imagine then, the value created and financial benefits you would gain by developing a self-driving mower powered by AI? While developing an AI-powered lawn mower is likely hard, the rewards will be directly attributed to the challenges involved.

But, how about if you develop a self-driving mower that uses AI that can mow the lawn? Imagine the value you can create by doing that and some of the financial benefits that go along with it. While developing the AI-powered lawn mower is likely hard, the rewards will be directly attributed to the challenges involved.

Struggle sharpens our skills in the process and fuels our growth. The learning journey is about overcoming obstacles, recognizing that struggle fuels growth and seeing the reward for doing so. When we overcome a struggle, we gain self-esteem, give value to others and experience satisfaction. Failing, getting back up and trying again and again is a key element of the learning journey.

Jimmy Butler, "Jimmy Buckets," of the Miami Heat knows a thing or two about struggle, perseverance and the hard work it takes to rebound from adversity. With an annual salary of nearly $49 million, he's one of the highest paid players in the National Basketball Association (NBA), but that success didn't come overnight.

Jimmy Butler had a rough upbringing. His father abandoned him and his mom when he was just an infant. He was raised by his mother until age 13 when she kicked him out of the house. With no parental figure in sight, he had to do a lot of things for himself that other kids took for granted. Butler had little stability in his life until he moved in with a friend's family, who already had seven kids, before his senior year of high school.

Believing in himself helped propel him through each challenge. Although Butler was a talented basketball player in high school and became an all-district player, he did not receive any scholarship offers from NCAA Division I college basketball programs. Disappointed but determined, Butler got back in the game and headed to junior college in Tyler, Texas to play basketball. He continued to perfect his craft, making many sacrifices along the way.

While at Tyler Junior College, his ability quickly caught the attention of NCAA Division I college scouts and he was recruited by Marquette University. This was a game changer in Jimmy Butler's life. Because of his talent and perseverance, Butler would eventually become an NBA draft pick and NBA Most Improved Player and All-Star and earn that 49-million-dollar paycheck.

SO, WHAT CAN BUTLER'S STORY TEACH MY KIDS ABOUT MONEY AND THE VALUE OF BEING GRITTY?

Sure, Butler's multimillion dollar salary is impressive, but what is even more impressive is the struggle getting there.

It doesn't matter if your child is an athlete or a mathlete. The difficult obstacles they face in pursuing a goal or passion is what ultimately makes their achievement fulfilling. You want to teach your kids to take on difficult tasks as the majority of people will shy away from them. With stories like Butler's, we can see that obstacles create true opportunities for growth and happiness.

As parents, we want our kids to be happy and content humans. The learning journey helps kids find that happiness and live fulfilling lives. It serves as a blueprint for achieving success in the game of life. The earlier your child grasps these principles, the sooner they will form their own systems of accountability that can easily become ingrained habits.

A caution to parents: Parents often struggle with letting their kids fail because they have an intense desire to protect them from any pain or disappointment, and because they may believe that constant intervention is necessary for their child's success. This overprotective approach can lead them to prioritize short-term comfort over the long-term benefits of learning from failures and developing resilience. Watching your kids struggle without stepping in is very difficult for any parent. However, don't rob them of this experience.

This journey acts as a guiding light when your child faces challenges, whether it is dealing with bullies, receiving a disappointing grade in school, not making the soccer team or being criticized by others.

When adversity comes knocking (and it always will), it presents a prime opportunity to sit down with your child and work through these challenges.

By instilling strong values related to the journey, you're

paving the way for numerous meaningful discussions about the sacrifices required to excel in any endeavor.

The correlation between the level of skill necessary and the difficulty of achievement becomes apparent. When a task is easy, it tends to be a common pursuit with limited rewards. By imparting these principles to your children, you're not only guiding them towards applying these lessons to their financial decisions but also to various aspects of their lives.

This process of overcoming challenges has a profound impact. First and foremost, it fosters the development of self-esteem. Overcoming hurdles and mastering a skill, especially when it requires significant effort, naturally instills a sense of self-worth and accomplishment. This, in turn, leads to pride in your achievements and a deep-seated happiness that arises from knowing that you've put in the hard work to reach your goals.

Conquering adversity creates a sense of momentum that's akin to building a muscle. You start with a light weight and then you work your way up to heavier weights. As you achieve your goals, you gain confidence and the motivation to tackle more significant challenges. It's a self-reinforcing cycle that perpetuates growth and self-improvement.

Over time, it's as though you're developing a superpower—the ability to conquer obstacles, pursue excellence and achieve remarkable success in all areas of your life. This not only benefits your financial well-being but also your personal development and overall quality of life.

WHAT'S THE CORE MESSAGE BEHIND THE LEARNING JOURNEY?

The idea is that if you develop a skill, you can create value and impact. Maybe you are an amazing computer programmer who creates software that solves lots of problems, therefore making a great impact that provides a lot of value. By doing that, you're going to be compensated accordingly.

Money is a measurement of our contribution, impact and value. There's no need to chase money. I did that at one time in my life. Take it from me, it doesn't work. Incredibly wealthy people never chase money—they create value and impact. If you study people that really created something significant, they didn't set out to make a lot of money. They set out to impact and change industries. The money followed.

For example:

- Jeff Bezos' goal in starting Amazon was to offer a wide range of products to customers at a convenient and competitive price.
- Mark Zuckerberg's objective for starting *Facebook* was to create a social networking platform to connect people and facilitate communication between friends.
- Oprah Winfrey's goal in starting *The Oprah Winfrey Show* was to create a talk show that would entertain, inspire and empower viewers while dealing with important and meaningful topics.

All of these entrepreneurs just happened to make (a lot of) money along the way while creating value. The money didn't come first. Instead, the value came first and then the money followed. While the learning journey applies to money, it's really a roadmap to success. We want our kids to be happy and content.

Money doesn't necessarily bring about happiness (there's a lot of miserable people out there that have a lot of money), but creating value brings a sense of fulfillment beyond what's in your bank account.

WHAT IS THE LEARNING JOURNEY?

1. Try
2. Learn
3. Fail
4. Persist
5. Expand and Elevate
6. Repeat with Consistency

The following is a snapshot of each of the six rules:

1. TRY

Try new things—especially if it's uncomfortable. Life's not about staying in our comfort zone. Research shows putting yourself in new and unfamiliar situations triggers a part of the brain that releases dopamine. That part of the brain is only activated when you see or experience new things.

Although most people typically don't enjoy the feeling of being uncomfortable, the challenge is getting past that. By doing so, you can grow and benefit from the discomfort. As a parent, you'll want to encourage your child to try different activities as you explain how those are an opportunity for growth. Life is not a win or lose game; it's a "try" game.

2. LEARN

By learning, you gradually increase your skill over time no matter what activity you are doing. The more you practice, the better you get. When parents give their kids money without them earning it, they are missing out on learning the trials and tribulations on what it takes to earn it. Essentially, the parents are robbing them of that elation a toddler feels as they learn to walk.

Learning is a key component to our existence. We should

never stop learning no matter what our age. Research shows the benefits of lifelong learning are coping with a fast-changing world, greater paychecks because of better job opportunities and living a more enriching and fulfilling life.

Sometimes kids think of learning as something they do inside the confines of school walls. To pique their interest in learning outside of school, make learning fun and relevant to their interests. Encourage their natural curiosity and let them take the lead in exploring topics they find interesting. We want to nurture kids who are naturally curious about life.

3. FAIL

Failure is a natural part of learning and life. I think Bill Gates said it best, "It's fine to celebrate success but it is more important to heed the lessons of failure." Failure is a natural part of scientific experiments, but isn't something highlighted often. It's all about making the big discovery. However, science inevitably must fail to achieve discovery.

Recently, my daughter failed a test. As a parent, it was an opportunity for me to illuminate what we can learn from failure. My daughter is a financial adviser working on earning her CFP® certification. Undoubtedly, the exam is tough. The 170-question test consists of two three-hour sessions over one day. My daughter finished both of those sessions in less than one hour and 45 minutes.

She was devastated when she failed the exam. Up to this point, she had never failed a test in her life. When she called me to share the news, I responded, "Failure is natural. Without failure, there is no success. You probably took the studying kind of light this first time. You can take it again and approach it in a different way."

She looked back at what happened and realized her error. The next time she took the test, she put in the work studying and on test day, she took her time and passed it easily. She learned a great lesson, but she needed to learn the pain of failure first.

4. PERSIST

Persistence is all about continuing to work toward a goal or maintain a particular course of action despite challenges, obstacles, setbacks or difficulties. It involves determination, tenacity and the willingness to push through the struggle.

Persistence allows you to maintain your motivation and commitment over an extended period, even in the face of failures or discouragement.

Persistent people are resilient and can bounce back from failures or setbacks. They view these challenges as learning opportunities and keep moving forward.

They also understand that achieving significant goals often takes time. Persistence involves the patience to continue working steadily toward the goal, even when progress may be slow.

That's why persistence is integral to the learning journey. When children learn tenacity, they are better able to adapt. They can modify their approach or strategy to whatever it is that they're working on to overcome obstacles or make improvements, thereby elevating themselves closer to success.

5. EXPAND AND ELEVATE

The cycle of attempting, learning, failing and persisting consistently leads to improvement because it is the core mechanism of skill development. Each attempt provides valuable insights, while failures highlight areas for growth and ways to improve. This process, repeated over time, naturally refine techniques and deepens understanding, regardless of what task you are doing.

Always take the initiative to expand and try to get better or more efficient at whatever skill you are working on.

It takes sacrifice and discipline to elevate to achieve success.

Ask Jimmy Butler, the NBA Superstar. Did he sacrifice a lot in his childhood to get there? You bet. Did it require incredible discipline? Sure. But, was the end result of becoming one of the best NBA players worth it? Absolutely.

The skill level and endurance required to become an NBA player is incredibly intense, even for the most talented athletes.

According to the National Collegiate Athletic Association (NCAA), just 1.2% of NCAA athletes make it to the NBA and just 0.03% of high school seniors that play basketball eventually get drafted by NBA franchises. The average player plays 4.5 years in the league. Butler has been in the league since 2011.

No matter what your child's goals or aspirations are, to be successful at it, they're going to have to be willing to sacrifice in some way or another. That sacrifice might be getting up early on the weekend to practice a sport when the rest of their friends are sleeping in or staying up late. It takes discipline. Olympic dreams require even more effort.

If your child has a goal of competing in the Olympics, you can have a candid talk with them about what amount of effort that would require. Let's say your child has a dream of becoming an Olympic figure skater. You'll want them to know how it's a challenging and competitive path to take.

Figure skaters must practice nearly every day for several hours both on and off the ice. Even if they had the talent, would they be willing to miss hanging out with friends and dedicating all this time to a sport they love knowing that they may never achieve their dream? And that dream doesn't even factor in the cost of coaching fees, travel expenses and athletic conditioning to keep the body operating at elite levels.

To illustrate how competitive it is, consider that the maximum number of entries for the 2024 Paris Winter Olympics in figure skating worldwide is 30 women, 30 men, 20 pairs and 24 ice dancing couples.

As a parent, you don't want to crush your child's dreams or aspirations. You simply want to explain in age-appropriate terms what sacrifices and dedication is required to achieve big Olympic dreams. And then clue them in on the stepping stones to get there.

Each gold medal Olympic figure skater starts the same way as any other novice skater—stepping on the ice for the first time. The process of getting good at something is a universal skill that creates value and is then directly tied to compensation. The better you are, the more you get paid, period.

The same applies to business owners, like the landscaper I mentioned who decides to develop AI-operated self-mowing lawn mowers. To expand and elevate as a business owner, you need to find the most efficient way to provide value to your customers to enhance your profitability. This kind of strategic thinking is all tied to the learning journey.

6. REPEAT WITH CONSISTENCY

Repetition is fundamental to achieving great things in life. The path to success is rarely a straightforward one, and it's often paved with challenges and setbacks. However, the ultimate reward, the sense of accomplishment, makes every struggle worthwhile.

This is like the way athletes continuously strive to improve. When they win a trophy, they don't rest on their laurels; they set their sights on what's next. Success is a never-ending journey. The goals may evolve, but the fundamental principles that guide us, the learning journey, remain constant and timeless.

Consistency is the linchpin of this process. It's about taking small, deliberate steps in a specific direction over an extended period. These incremental efforts accumulate over time, leading to significant gains. But, if these steps aren't realistic, you simply won't continue as it becomes so hard to do. Similar to an athlete that hones their skills and refines their technique through relentless practice, in the pursuit of success, we must persistently repeat our actions, learn from our experiences, and adapt to new challenges.

Somebody new to running shouldn't set an unrealistic goal of running 35 miles a week to begin their new regimen. Chances are, if they attempt such a feat they will get injured, quit and never attempt running again. Instead, they should start small by aiming to do something more realistic like running a quarter of a mile four days a week. At first, it might not seem like a lofty enough goal. However, as they begin to increase their mileage just a little bit each time, soon that quarter mile turns into a half mile and then a mile. If they consistently run four days a week, eventually six to nine months down the road, by building a consistent habit, it creates momentum and eventually that goal of running 35 miles a week becomes realistic and attainable.

Whether in the realm of finance, personal growth or any other aspect of life, the concept of repetition and consistency remains a universal truth. It pushes us closer to our desired achievements making the journey all the more fulfilling.

WHAT'S THE BIGGEST TAKEAWAY FROM THE LEARNING JOURNEY?

The biggest takeaway is if your kids put in the effort, they will receive a reward for doing so. Effort equals reward. When kids understand that putting in effort and working hard leads to rewards and positive outcomes, they become more inclined to persevere, set goals and develop a strong work ethic. Self-motivation, self-improvement and self-discipline are the path to happiness and self-fulfillment.

The following are some tips to make following the learning journey more engaging for your children:

Lead by Example: Children often look up to their parents and want to emulate them. If you want your kids to embrace learning, start by showing your own interest in learning. Whether it's a sport, a board game or any other activity, play it enthusiastically and make it a part of your routine.

Join Them: Make learning a shared experience. Engage in an activity together, whether it's a friendly match in a sport, a family game night or any other rule-based endeavor. The act of doing an activity together will not only teach them but also create memorable family moments.

Encourage Questions: Encourage your kids to ask questions. When they show curiosity or confusion, take the time to explain and simplify what you are teaching them. This will show them that you are invested in their understanding and development.

Find a Coach: If you're not proficient in a particular activity, consider finding a coach or instructor. This way, your children can benefit from learning from an expert and you can both follow their guidance. This will also show your dedication to their growth.

Use Positive Reinforcement: Teach your children about the concept of effort and reward. Linking rewards to their efforts can help children understand the connection between hard work and positive outcomes. Rewards can be small, such as extra playtime, a special treat or privileges like choosing a family activity. Be sure to reward their progress with encouragement and positive feedback.

Praise Effort, Not Just the End Result: Instead of solely focusing on the outcome, recognize and praise the effort your child puts into tasks. This helps them understand that hard work and perseverance are valued, regardless of the end result.

Make Learning Fun: Inject an element of fun into the learning process. Create challenges, competitions or rewards for mastering something. This gamification can make the learning process more enjoyable for kids.

Variety: Introduce your children to a variety of activities with different kinds of rules. This can help them discover their interests and expand their knowledge of different rule systems.

Patience and Persistence: Understand that it may take time for your kids to grasp and appreciate certain concepts. Be patient and persistent in your efforts. Avoid putting too much pressure on them and allow them to learn at their own pace.

Celebrate Success: When your children demonstrate an understanding of new concepts and apply them in the game or activity, celebrate their successes. This positive reinforcement will motivate them to continue learning.

Keep it Lighthearted: While it's essential to teach the importance of learning new things, remember to keep the atmosphere lighthearted and enjoyable. Avoid turning it into a strict or stressful experience. The goal is to foster a love for learning.

Find a Community of Like-minded Parents: You can share your resources and experiences with each other. Connecting with others in similar situations helps combat isolation, enriches the learning experience, and creates a sense of belonging.

Start with Age-appropriate Tasks: Begin by assigning simple tasks suitable for your child's age and capabilities. For example, cleaning up toys, completing homework or helping with household chores. Emphasize that when they put in effort and complete these tasks, they will earn rewards or privileges. These rewards don't need to be big, and of course, there might be some baseline tasks where they aren't rewarded. In doing so however, you are setting up the concept that "if you do this, you get this."

Set Clear Goals and Expectations: Clearly explain all the expectations are for each task and discuss the outcome or rewards that will follow their efforts. Breaking goals into smaller, manageable steps will help children see progress and stay motivated.

Be Consistent: Consistency is key when teaching any concept to a child. Reinforce the effort and reward system consistently, and follow through with promised rewards to build trust and reinforce the desired behavior.

By incorporating these tips, you can help instill in your kids a genuine interest in learning new things. It can also make the learning process an enjoyable and valuable experience for the whole family.

HOW CAN YOU GET KIDS MORE EXCITED ABOUT THE LEARNING JOURNEY?

Your kids most likely follow certain celebrities and influencers. Most kids do. Even bringing up this topic provides teachable moments when it comes to money. Ask them about a celebrity or influencer they admire.

If your kid is a Swiftie, talk about how Taylor Swift achieved superstar status. Here's a little background: Swift was born in

West Reading, Pennsylvania, and despite her striking appearance, she was bullied because of her curly hair and desire to be a country singer.

That didn't stop her from pursuing her dream. She and her mom went to Nashville to pitch her demo-record with a negative response. Even so, she kept honing her skills.

When she was 13, her family uprooted their lives and moved near Nashville so she could pursue her dream. The next year, Swift signed a deal with Sony/ATV as a songwriter and became the youngest signing in the company's history.

Although Swift's success looked instant to most people, it wasn't. When she encountered disappointment, she continued to learn and grow.

In 2009, Kanye West protested her VMA award as she took the stage, which was a blow to her self-esteem. Kanye later mentioned her in a song without her permission, causing a he-said, she-said debate and a media and public backlash so great that she went completely MIA for over a year.

However, Swift emerged stronger than ever with her *Reputation* album, taking her power back. Much later, she took a hard situation—losing her master recordings with her former record label—and turned it into a success by rerecording her albums and reaping the financial rewards and musical acclaim.

Beyond her music, Swift does a lot of philanthropic work and charitable acts for her fans, much of which is not publicized directly by her or her team. For example, during her Eras Tour, she donated money to food banks in every city she performed. Her value and impact is through her songwriting and her music, but also through how she helps others. Today, Swift is a 12-time Grammy Award winner and has an estimated net worth of $1.1 billion.

Conversations like this about Swift and others illustrate the time and effort it takes to achieve great success—these wins don't happen overnight or without struggle. This is an opportunity to discuss with your child about how commitment and discipline have a direct proportion to the amount of money that you can make regardless of your upbringing or environment.

Everybody goes through times of success and disappointment. It's your ability to stick with it and learn from those failures that allows you to get better. Failure is just as important as success because it shows you where your weaknesses are and offers clues on how to correct them. Getting better creates value, impact and money naturally follow. Our kids need to know that money is a measurement game, not a "thing" game. It's dangerous when people only see money as a mechanism to buy things.

SHOULD PARENTS EXPECT SOME PUSHBACK FROM THEIR KIDS?

Adhering to the learning journey can be challenging at times, like when your kid doesn't want to do their homework, go to school or do some other activity. When teaching your kids, recognize it will get difficult. To cope, parents should stay patient, try different approaches and break lessons into smaller parts while leading by example and acknowledging difficulties. It's also helpful to celebrate small victories, remembering that the goal is long-term learning and growth.

As a parent, you want to distill early on that there's a relationship between effort and achieving a goal. To excel as an athlete, musician, scholar or anything else, you need to put in the necessary effort. It's the consistent repetition that makes the learning journey part of your child's DNA.

And you're not off the hook if you weren't taught these principles as a child—you still have to teach your kids. Take it from Richard Williams, father of tennis champions Venus and Serena Williams. He had never played tennis, but his vision for his daughters helped to propel them toward greatness.

After seeing Romanian tennis player Virginia Ruzici win the 1978 French Open and take home $20,000, Williams came up with a 78-page plan for his daughters to become tennis pros and became their coach. Richard taught himself how to play and coach tennis by watching instructional videos.

Because Williams had no preconceived notions about the best way to play tennis, he wasn't afraid to challenge the system. And he did. He argued that you could get back into the court much faster by having an open stance versus a closed stance. The tennis professionals disagreed, noting someone couldn't generate enough power to do so. Venus and Serena Williams proved them wrong.

Richard Williams was a sponge for learning and was on a mission to find the most efficient way to play tennis. He wasn't afraid to go against convention. He had nothing to lose and everything to gain. That's what the learning journey is about— possibility. The possibility of *what if?*

Never forget that you are your child's mentor when it comes to the learning journey. You can easily teach the principles in this book to your child. It doesn't matter whether you are rich, poor or somewhere in between.

And remember, you are doing a huge disservice to your kids if you don't teach your kids the rules *and* allow them to fail. This concept really comes into play when it comes to money. If you are just handing your kids money or ignoring the topic of money altogether, you aren't doing them any favors. Failing is part of the process.

Teaching your kids that there is always a next goal, even after failure, is an essential lesson in nurturing their growth and development. It instills a sense of ambition, resilience and continuous improvement.

By emphasizing the idea that each accomplishment is a stepping stone toward the next challenge, you empower your kids to maintain a growth mindset and view setbacks as opportunities for growth.

This not only encourages perseverance but it also teaches them the importance of setting goals and working toward them throughout their lives. This fosters a sense of purpose and optimism, as they realize that there is always something new to achieve on their journey of self-discovery.

In the next chapter, we'll focus on the five faces of a dollar, which will reinforce everything they've learned from the learning journey.

———

KEY TAKEAWAYS

- Creating impact and value build self esteem and happiness.
- At the end of the day, it's about learning to create value out in the world. Compensation will follow.
- Teaching your kids that there is always a next goal is an essential lesson in nurturing their growth and development.
- The more effort you invest in a task, the greater the subsequent reward tends to be.
- Struggle is an essential part of learning. Without the struggle, there are no rewards. As parents, you need to allow your kids to struggle and even fail, so they can become more resilient. Encourage them to be gritty kids.
- An easy childhood can produce a hard life while a hard childhood can produce an easy life.
- Download the Learning Journey Worksheet at www.401kid.education.

CHAPTER 4

THE POWER OF EARLY HABITS—WHY IT'S CRUCIAL TO INSTILL POSITIVE HABITS IN YOUR KIDS

"We know habits matter; we just need more good habits and fewer bad ones."
—BJ Fogg, author of *Tiny Habits*

LESSON: VALUES PLUS CONSISTENT HABITS CAN CREATE AN AMAZING life. Forming good habits in childhood lays a strong foundation for lifelong success, and delaying these teachings can make it harder for children to thrive as adults.

Popular Stanford behavioral scientist BJ Fogg was on the right track when he said, "Take a behavior you want, make it tiny, find where it fits naturally in your life, and nurture its growth. If you want to create long-term change, it's best to start small."[1]

Fogg's idea is to create a constellation of habits, tiny in size but big on impact. As humans, we are creatures of habit. We have habits around eating, exercising and leisure activities. Our kids are automatically forming habits too—whether it's how much time they spend on their screens, on social media, playing video games or outdoor activities.

Developing positive habits from a young age influences positive outcomes in adulthood. Positive habits carve a pathway to self-improvement, fostering a journey marked by dedication, consistency and growth.

In contrast, negative habits often lead to a decline in mental well-being creating a web of challenges that hinder progress. As parents, you want to be a good role model to your kids. If you don't take on this role, others will establish their path for them.

Children often struggle to navigate the confusing ways in which the ever-changing world presents itself. This lack of direction occurs on a moment-to-moment basis, furthering their confusion. You want to create stability so you set a foundation for your child's habits now and into the future. The early years of a child's life are a time of wonder, growth and constant learning.

These formative years are more than just a phase of development; they serve as the blueprint for adulthood. Parents play a pivotal role in shaping their children's future through sharing positive habits and values early on.

WHY IS IT SO CRUCIAL TO INSTILL THESE HABITS AT AN EARLY AGE, RATHER THAN WAITING UNTIL ADOLESCENCE OR BEYOND?

From birth through childhood, a child's brain undergoes incredible growth, making early development a critical window of opportunity for forming habits. Neuroscience shows us that a child's brain is highly "plastic," meaning it is adaptable and easily shaped by experiences.

During this period, neural connections are forming at a rapid pace, which makes it easier to instill habits that will last a lifetime. The habits formed during these crucial years become a part of the brain's wiring, affecting everything from decision-making to emotional responses.

When a child repeats a behavior, their brain strengthens the neural pathways associated with that action, making it easier for them to engage in that behavior again. Whether it's brushing their teeth, saying "please" and "thank you," or saving a portion of their allowance, positive repetition during early childhood makes these actions more automatic.

For instance, teaching a child to regularly clean up their toys may seem like a small habit, but over time, it builds a foundation of responsibility and discipline. When they encounter bigger tasks later in life, the habit of being organized and responsible has already been deeply ingrained.

Delaying the introduction of positive habits can mean missed opportunities for optimal brain development. As children grow older, the brain becomes less plastic, meaning it is more difficult to form new, healthy behaviors or rewire established patterns. This is why habits developed early are more likely to stick, while negative habits picked up in later years are harder to break.

DO EARLY HABITS BUILD A FOUNDATION FOR FUTURE BEHAVIOR?

Imagine instilling the habit of saving money in a child from a young age. Starting with something as simple as putting a portion of their allowance into a piggy bank teaches them delayed gratification and financial responsibility.

Over time, this seemingly small act compounds into a foundational understanding of saving and managing finances. It's similar to encouraging kids to read daily, which fosters a love of learning, and compounds into better academic performance and intellectual curiosity.

Early habits are like small seeds. When watered consistently, they grow into towering trees that provide lifelong benefits. Whether it's a habit of practicing kindness, staying organized or taking care of their health, these actions build a child's character and set the stage for a successful future.

Habits formed early on often stay with people for the rest of their lives. As kids transition into adolescence and adulthood, their day-to-day actions are influenced by what they've learned in their younger years. If positive habits such as self-discipline, patience, and critical thinking are already in place, they become valuable tools in navigating the more complex challenges that come with growing older.

On the flip side, habits of procrastination, impulsive behavior, or neglecting responsibilities, if established early, can follow a person into adulthood, limiting their potential and success. The question then becomes: do we want to nurture habits that serve our kids well in the future, or leave them to develop behaviors that might hold them back?

HOW EASY IS IT TO UNLEARN NEGATIVE HABITS THAT YOU'VE LEARNED AS A KID?

Once negative patterns become ingrained, they can be very difficult to unlearn. Research shows that it takes much more time and effort to break a bad habit than to develop a good one. This is why early intervention is so crucial—by instilling positive habits early on, parents can avoid the uphill battle of trying to undo negative behaviors later in life.

Unlearning negative habits can also have emotional costs. For example, a child who was never taught emotional regulation might struggle with frustration or anger later in life. This may lead to struggles with relationships, academic performance or career success.

WHAT ARE SOME OF THOSE LONG-TERM BENEFITS OF LEARNING POSITIVE HABITS EARLY ON?

Good habits early on translate into better academic outcomes. Children who develop strong study habits and time-management skills are more likely to excel in school. These academic successes can carry forward into professional life, where discipline, focus and a strong work ethic often distinguish top performers from the rest. Early habits of curiosity, learning and resilience prepare kids to succeed in an increasingly complex and competitive world.

The long-term benefits of early habit formation aren't just limited to academics or careers—they extend to emotional well-being and social success. Habits such as kindness, empathy and communication skills help kids navigate their social world with confidence. These habits lead to deeper relationships and a strong social support network, which is crucial for happiness and fulfillment.

One area that early habit formation can have a particularly profound effect on is financial stability. If children are taught the value of money, saving and investing from a young age, they are more likely to grow into adults who make wise financial decisions. A kid who learns the habit of budgeting early on is less likely to struggle with debt or impulse spending as an adult.

When kids are taught to consistently act in certain ways, they begin to internalize the values behind those actions. For instance, a kid who is regularly encouraged to share their toys or invite others to play learns the value of generosity and inclusion. These values become part of their identity, influencing their moral compass and guiding their behavior throughout life.

Parents often hope their children will grow up with strong character traits like honesty, resilience and kindness. These traits don't appear out of nowhere; they are built through repeated actions—habits—that reflect those values.

Kids are always observing the adults in their lives. Parents who model positive habits—whether it's maintaining a budget, sticking to a daily exercise routine, or treating others with respect—set an example for their kids to follow. Consistency in behavior from parents reinforces the importance of these habits.

Consistency also plays a major role in forming habits. It's not enough to teach a kid something once and expect it to stick. Repetition and reinforcement are key to ensuring that a habit becomes second nature. The more a kid practices positive behavior, the more likely it is to become a permanent part of their life.

Sharing daily routines with your kids not only helps kids develop good habits but also creates lasting memories and a sense of security. Whether it's a morning routine, family reading time, or a shared savings goal, these moments strengthen the relationship between you and your kids while also fostering life-long habits.

The habits we instill in our children early on are some of the greatest gifts we can give them. By starting early, we take advantage of their brain's incredible capacity for learning, set them up for future success, and help them build character traits that will carry them through life.

As parents, our job is to lay the groundwork by teaching these habits consistently, patiently and lovingly. The habits kids learn early on don't just benefit them in childhood; they echo throughout their entire lives, helping them navigate the world with confidence, wisdom and resilience.

WHAT ARE THE POSITIVE PHYSICAL AND MENTAL HEALTH BENEFITS OF BUILDING CONSCIENTIOUS, HEALTHY HABITS OVER UNHEALTHY ONES?

Developing healthy habits early in life sets the stage for children to become successful, resilient and well-adjusted adults. Habits are the small, consistent actions and decisions that shape the way we live. For children, habits are particularly important because they create the foundation for long-term physical, emotional and mental well-being. Moreover, the earlier these habits are formed, the more automatic and ingrained they become.

Building conscientious, healthy habits versus unhealthy ones is critical for several reasons. It influences children's health, decision-making, academic and social success, emotional regulation and overall sense of purpose and achievement. One of the most obvious but often overlooked reasons for instilling healthy habits in children is the direct impact these habits have on both physical and mental health. When children learn the importance of taking care of their bodies and minds, they establish behaviors that prevent a host of physical and mental health issues later in life.

Children who learn to eat balanced meals, exercise regularly and get adequate sleep are far more likely to avoid conditions like obesity, type 2 diabetes, heart disease and other chronic illnesses. Simple habits like brushing teeth, washing hands and limiting junk food consumption can seem minor in the short term, but they have long-term health implications.

For example, establishing a habit of daily physical activity, whether it's through organized sports or simple play, sets the stage for a lifetime of movement. This habit helps maintain a healthy weight, improves cardiovascular health, strengthens bones and muscles and reduces the risk of diseases.

Mental health is also influenced by daily habits. Children who develop routines that include mindfulness, play, and creativity tend to have better mental health outcomes. Learning to cope with stress, manage emotions and take time for relaxation is crucial. For example, teaching children relaxation techniques, such as breathing exercises or yoga, can help them manage anxiety and stress, reducing the likelihood of developing mental health issues like depression or chronic anxiety later in life.

Unhealthy habits, on the other hand, such as overeating, avoiding physical activity, and poor sleep patterns, can lead to physical ailments and mental health struggles. These unhealthy habits may become harder to break as children grow older.

Conscientious habits build self-discipline, one of the most important life skills a child can develop. Self-discipline helps children delay gratification, work toward long-term goals and resist distractions or temptations that can derail their progress.

One of the most significant benefits of self-discipline is learning the concept of delayed gratification—the ability to wait for a future reward rather than seeking immediate satisfaction.

Research, such as the famous Stanford marshmallow experiment, has shown that children who can delay gratification tend to have better life outcomes, including higher academic achievement, better health and stronger relationships.

By teaching children healthy habits like saving money, finishing their homework before playing and practicing a skill regularly, parents are helping them understand that success often comes from consistent effort over time. Children who learn this will be better equipped to manage their time, make smart financial decisions and pursue their goals without being derailed by short-term desires.

In contrast, unhealthy habits can foster impulsive behavior, where children seek immediate pleasure or relief from discomfort without considering the long-term consequences. For example, a child who habitually procrastinates or frequently chooses screen time over studying may struggle with academic performance and fall behind. Over time, the inability to delay gratification can lead to poor decision-making, including impulsive financial choices or unhealthy lifestyle habits as adults.

Kid's habits influence their future success, whether academically, professionally, or personally. Success is rarely the result of one-time decisions or actions; instead, it's the accumulation of small, positive choices repeated over time. Healthy habits like time management, goal-setting and perseverance are essential for achieving long-term success.

Teaching children habits of responsibility, such as doing chores, organizing their schoolwork, or managing their time effectively, helps them develop a sense of accountability and ownership over their tasks. Time management is a critical skill that children can use throughout their lives, whether it's for succeeding in school, managing work responsibilities or balancing personal commitments.

When children are taught to break tasks into manageable steps, they learn to set realistic goals and meet deadlines. This also fosters a sense of pride and accomplishment when they see their hard work pay off.

Healthy habits also instill a sense of perseverance, or "grit," which is the ability to push through challenges. When children regularly engage in habits like practicing a musical instrument, studying for tests or working on a hobby, they learn that improvement comes with effort over time. This resilience will help them tackle bigger challenges in life, whether it's applying for jobs, managing finances or navigating relationships.

Unhealthy habits like avoiding difficult tasks, giving up easily, or not following through with commitments can lead to a mindset of complacency or defeat. These behaviors can hinder children's potential and prevent them from achieving their goals.

Developing healthy habits extends beyond personal responsibility and includes how children interact with others. Building good social habits—such as being kind, practicing empathy, and communicating effectively—helps children form strong, positive relationships with peers, teachers and family members.

Teaching children the habit of considering others' feelings and showing kindness helps them develop empathy. This is critical for building lasting relationships, as empathetic children are more likely to collaborate with others, resolve conflicts peacefully and make meaningful connections. Habits like sharing, listening actively and helping others build a foundation for strong, supportive relationships.

Healthy communication habits—such as being honest, speaking respectfully, and managing emotions—equip children to navigate social situations with ease. These habits ensure that they can express themselves clearly while also understanding the perspectives of others. As they grow older, these skills become invaluable in personal relationships, the workplace and broader social contexts.

In contrast, unhealthy habits like selfishness, dishonesty or aggression can lead to social isolation and difficulty maintaining friendships. Children who struggle to regulate their emotions or fail to consider others' needs may face challenges in building strong, positive relationships.

Healthy habits help children develop a growth mindset—the belief that abilities and intelligence can be developed through effort and perseverance. When children engage in habits that encourage learning, persistence and curiosity, they start to see challenges as opportunities for growth rather than obstacles.

One of the most important aspects of a growth mindset is understanding that failure is part of the learning process. Children who are encouraged to try new things, take risks and view mistakes as learning experiences are more likely to develop resilience and adaptability.

WHAT'S THE BEST WAY FOR A PARENT TO GUIDE A CHILD?

Learning discipline and delayed gratification are two of the most important skills when it comes to forming good habits. To help your child grasp the concept of delayed gratification, explain how it's like planting seeds. You've got these tiny seeds of potential in your hand which you choose to plant and nurture into something extraordinary.

Delayed gratification refers to the capacity to resist the temptation of immediate rewards, like deciding between eating one cookie now or three cookies after waiting several hours.

In this cookie scenario, your child has the freedom to select their preferred choice—eat it now or wait. Similar to the gradual development of a muscle, this ability to wait requires patience and time to strengthen.

Discipline is waking up every morning and doing the work, no excuses. It's about sticking to the plan even when you'd rather take the easy way out. It's not always glamorous—it's often mundane—but it's what separates the dreamers from the doers.

Patience gained from delayed gratification fuels discipline, which is your shield against distractions. It keeps you on track knowing what's waiting at the end of the road is worth far more than instant gratification.

Developing skills isn't just a checklist; it's a journey. It's about the sweat, tears, frustrations and triumphs. Real growth happens when you embrace it. Let delayed gratification and discipline be your guiding lights.

Trust me, as you navigate this journey with your child, the skills they learn will allow them to transform into someone capable of achieving their wildest dreams. It's not just about the destination—it's about relishing every step of the way.

Today, our kids have more distractions than ever to take their attention away from their goals. Advertising is always selling the value of *now, now, now!* This is a trap designed to steal your money.

Money is like a special ruler we use to measure how much something means to us. Just like inches or centimeters help us measure length, money helps us measure the value of things we want. If something has a big impact or is super important, it might cost more money.

Money habits are intrinsically tied to our values. We need to teach our kids that the work they do is all about value creation. We send our kids to school so they can become value creators.

The value becomes their *why*. But what follows is often overlooked. You can become a great value creator, but a poor money manager. You want to avoid that.

I had a friend who had a public net worth of $300 million but never had any money. He was in a lot of legal trouble when we first met. I asked him, "Where's the money?" He had no clue.

His CPA and I did an audit over the last three years and discovered he never saved any money. Sure, he made a lot of money, but whatever money came in, he spent it all. Having a mansion, multiple luxury vehicles or several homes is not a bad thing, but it's imperative to know if your cash flow is in balance with your net worth.

While my friend understood value creation as he was incredibly talented, he never learned financial competency. While he was no stranger to sacrifice and discipline in his career, he didn't apply it to other aspects of his life including his chosen lifestyle. My friend is a perfect example of why you want to have consistent money conversations with your child. Or as Shaquille O'Neal would say, "Making money is easy, keeping it is hard." My friend lacked financial discipline because he never learned it when he was younger.

Just as trees take years to grow to their full height, money conversations will yield gradual and steady progress rather than elicit immediate results. Meaningful accomplishments require a sustained effort.

As your child's most important mentor, you are going to help them build healthy habits when it comes to money even if your parents didn't do that for you.

Along the way, you'll be incentivizing them with rewards just like companies entice employees with their 401K plans by matching their investment. While you won't be opening up a 401K account for them per se, you will be teaching them about investing and saving in ways they can relate to so they can watch their money grow.

By teaching your kids about delayed gratification, and the importance of sacrifice and discipline, you are essentially giving them the keys to a life full of freedom.

Unlike many of their peers, your children won't need to be in bondage to the ever-changing wants and demands of a lifestyle they can't keep up with. Creating consistent money conversations with your child can simplify the concept of money.

ANY IDEAS ON HOW TO KEEP MONEY CONVERSATIONS TOP OF MIND?

Consistency is key when it comes to money discussions. What that consistency looks like for you may vary depending on your situation. Maybe once a week or once a month you have family financial insight conversations. Do what works best for you.

To help give you different ideas, I've created the following "Money Matters" weekly calendar to encourage families to have those vital money discussions. Choose one of the following:

MONDAY

Game Night: Play finance-themed games like Monopoly, The Game of Life or Cashflow for Kids.

TUESDAY

Savings Day: Review savings goals together or make deposits to savings accounts.

WEDNESDAY

Entrepreneur Hour: Brainstorm business ideas or work on ongoing entrepreneurial projects.

THURSDAY

Budget Buddy Time: Involve kids in household budgeting or planning for upcoming expenses.

FRIDAY

Financial Story Time: Read books with financial themes or discuss money-related news articles.

SATURDAY

Real-World Money Day: Practice using money in real situations (grocery shopping, garage sales, etc.).

SUNDAY

Giving and Gratitude: Discuss charitable giving, volunteer or express gratitude for what you have.

Feel free to adjust the calendar based on your family's schedule and interests. The calendar is a good reminder to keep those money conversations going consistently with your kids.

The Ramirez family were eager to try out the "Money Matters" family calendar when they noticed their kids Sophia, 12, and Luis, 9, were getting swayed by social media influencers in ways that didn't match the family values.

On Mondays, they played Monopoly, with Sofia surprising everyone with her strategic property investments. Tuesdays became a favorite as the kids eagerly counted their savings, with Luis proudly announcing he was halfway to his goal of buying a new bike. Wednesday's Entrepreneur Hour sparked creativity. Sofia started a small jewelry-making business, while Luis offered dog-walking services in the neighborhood.

As weeks passed, the family noticed significant changes. During Thursday's Budget Buddy Time, the kids suggested ways of cutting household expenses. Friday's Financial Story Time opened discussions about historical events like the Great Depression, broadening their perspective on money's role in society. Saturday's real-world money experiences at the local farmer's market taught them about value and negotiation. And on Sundays, they found joy in selecting charities to support, fostering a sense of gratitude and social responsibility.

Within months, Sofia and Luis were making more thoughtful

spending decisions, setting ambitious savings goals and even teaching their friends about money. The Ramirez parents were amazed at how their simple calendar had not only improved their children's financial literacy but had also brought the family closer together through shared learning and open discussions about money.

KEY TAKEAWAYS

- If you don't teach your kids how to establish positive habits, somebody else will.
- Delayed gratification and discipline are keys to building good money habits.
- There's a process to building healthy habits.
- Money is a measurement of value.
- Download the Consistency Calendar at www.401kid.education.

CHAPTER 5

THE FIRST PAYCHECK: THE FOUNDATION OF FINANCIAL DISCIPLINE

"Because of what I did when I was 10 years old, I'm not living from paycheck to paycheck, and I can do things because I want to do them."
—Macaulay Culkin

LESSON: WITHOUT FINANCIAL DISCIPLINE, NO AMOUNT OF INCOME will ever be enough.

Receiving our first paycheck holds a special place in our lives. It's not just money; it's a tangible reward for the skills we've developed, the knowledge we've acquired and the value we've created in our work. It's a moment of pride, but it also signals a crucial shift. This is when the journey toward financial independence truly begins.

It's easy to feel a rush of excitement when you receive that first paycheck, but the reality sets in quickly. Taxes are deducted, and what you see on paper is not what you take home. You're left with the net amount, and now comes the challenge—what do you do with what's left? When you break it down, you have four basic choices with any paycheck.

WHAT ARE THE FOUR CHOICES FOR PAYCHECKS?

When you break it down, you have four basic choices with any paycheck. You can save it for future needs, spend it on your current lifestyle, invest it to grow wealth or give some of it away. Each of these decisions directly impacts your financial future. The balance you strike between these four choices will shape your long-term financial health. The key takeaway is that without financial discipline, no amount of income will ever be enough.

Too often, we fall into the trap of thinking that more money will solve our problems. But the reality is that more money without discipline often leads to more problems, not fewer. This is where lifestyle inflation comes into play.

WHAT IS LIFESTYLE INFLATION?

Lifestyle inflation creeps up quietly. As we earn more, our wants grow. We justify bigger expenses because we believe we've "earned it." It's natural—we all have a baseline standard of living, but it tends to shift upward as our income increases. The danger is that if our spending grows at the same pace as our income, we will never build a financial cushion to achieve financial freedom.

We all have two baselines: the actual baseline—how much we are really spending—and the wish list baseline—the lifestyle we aspire to or believe we deserve. The gap between these two baselines is where most people get into trouble. We think we're spending within our means, but often, we aren't tracking the full picture.

For example, my daughter recently came to me frustrated because she couldn't figure out why she was accumulating credit card debt despite feeling like she had enough income to cover her expenses. In her mind, she had a budget and believed she had plenty of disposable income. But reality painted a different picture. She wasn't tracking her actual spending. It turned out that small, seemingly harmless purchases—like frequent Door-Dash orders and drinks—were adding up. Individually, they didn't feel excessive, but collectively, they were pushing her budget into the red.

Once she took the time to download her transactions and track her spending, she had an "aha" moment. The gap between her mental budget and her actual spending was glaringly clear. It wasn't a pleasant realization, but it was a necessary one. Financial discipline isn't always easy, and it sometimes requires facing uncomfortable truths, but this is the critical first step.

This experience led my daughter to an essential financial skill: tracking. It's not enough to set a budget and assume you're sticking to it. You need to measure your spending regularly, compare it to your budget, and adjust as needed. If you don't track your progress, you can't improve. This is true in every area of life, but especially in finances.

Imagine going out for a run without tracking your pace, distance, or time. It would be frustrating because you'd have no sense of how you're doing or how to improve. The same applies to managing your finances. If you don't track your income and expenses, it's impossible to know whether you're on the right path.

This brings us to the key metric for long-term financial success: free cash flow.

WHAT IS FREE CASH FLOW?

Free cash flow is the amount of money you have left after covering all of your expenses. It's the single most important number in personal finance and the heart of financial stability. Without free cash flow, there is no room to save or invest, which means there is no path to financial independence. If you spend every dollar you earn, it doesn't matter how large your income is

—you won't have the financial cushion to weather life's uncertainties, let alone build wealth for the future.

In business, free cash flow is a critical measure of health. Companies use it to determine whether they can invest in growth, pay dividends, or survive tough times. For families and individuals, it serves the same purpose. It's the excess cash that gives you options: to save, to invest, to give and to live with less financial stress.

As you advance in your career and earn more money, the key is ensuring your expenses don't rise at the same pace as your income. The temptation will always be to buy a bigger house, a nicer car or more stuff, but the goal is to balance the satisfaction of today's desires against our future financial future of tomorrow.

The equation is simple: income minus expenses equals free cash flow. This is the number that matters most in your financial life. If you have no free cash flow, the rest of this book—along with any discussions about saving, investing, or wealth-building—becomes pointless. You must first figure out a way to spend less than you earn so you can create free cash flow.

Many people fall into the trap of thinking they don't make enough money to save or invest. They convince themselves that their financial struggles will be solved by earning more, but this is an illusion. No matter how much you make, without discipline, you will always feel like you don't have enough. It's not about income—it's about how you manage the income you have.

Think about the people you see buying lottery tickets. Many of them spend hundreds of dollars on tickets every year, hoping for that one big payout. They might believe they don't have enough money to save, but the reality is that they do. It's just a matter of prioritizing how they spend.

WHAT'S THE BEST WAY TO PRACTICE FINANCIAL DISCIPLINE?

Keep in mind that financial discipline is not a one-time task. It's a lifelong practice. You need to track your spending, adjust your budget as your life changes and constantly reassess your goals. And while this may seem like a sterile, numbers-driven process, it's incredibly powerful. It gives you control over your future and the ability to navigate life with confidence.

Think of financial discipline like training for a marathon. You wouldn't just run without knowing your pace, distance or progress. You'd set goals, track your performance and work toward improving over time. Financial discipline works the same way. It's about setting goals, measuring your progress and making adjustments as needed.

When it comes to money, many of us avoid tracking or analyzing our finances because it forces us to face uncomfortable truths. We may feel embarrassed or ashamed, which leads us to ignore the problem in hopes it will somehow resolve itself. But that's a losing strategy. Facing your financial reality takes courage and vulnerability, and it's the first step toward meaningful change.

My daughter felt deeply embarrassed when she saw the reality of her spending, and it was difficult for her to admit it. But once she faced the truth, she found it liberating. She realized, "I don't really need that double latte every morning. I can do a better job at meal prep." It wasn't about depriving herself—it was about taking responsibility for her spending and feeling better about her choices. There is no worse feeling than financial irresponsibility.

KEY TAKEAWAYS

- When you are willing to get vulnerable and real about your finances, you can start building a solid financial foundation for the future.
- When you earn that first paycheck, it might be the first time you've received a tangible reward for the value you've created in your work.
- You can save your paycheck for future needs, spend it on your current lifestyle, invest it to grow wealth or give some of it away.

CHAPTER 6

BEYOND SPENDING: EXPLAINING MONEY'S MULTIPLE ROLES TO KIDS

"Too many people spend money they earned...to buy things they don't want...to impress people that they don't like."
—Will Rogers

LESSON: TEACH THE MULTIFACETED NATURE OF MONEY TO CHILDREN by highlighting its potential for earning, spending, saving and investing.

I created something called "The Five Faces of the Dollar" which is extremely helpful in showing kids the power of money, not in just its purchasing power, but what it can provide us if we choose to invest.

The Five Faces of the Dollar are:

1. Learn and Earn
2. Enjoy and Spend
3. Save
4. Invest for Future Freedom
5. Give and Share

1. LEARN AND EARN

The concept of earning is pretty simple to learn—you do something, and you get paid for it. Long before your child officially enters the workforce, as their parent and mentor, you can teach them the power of earning and how that can lead to financial independence.

Here are some tips for doing so:

Start with the Basics: Begin by explaining that money is earned by going to a job or providing a service. Help your kids understand that money is not just given freely but requires effort; it's not like getting a participation trophy for just showing up. For example, you could reward them for getting an improved grade on their report card. Allowances are also an easy way to teach your kids how to generate earned income by completing chores.

Set Clear Expectations: Create a list of age-appropriate tasks or chores that your child can accomplish to earn money. Clearly explain the tasks, how much money they will earn once they complete the task, and the quality of work you expect. Ensure that complex tasks have higher rewards than simple tasks. This helps your child understand the connection between input and the reward they will receive.

Encourage Entrepreneurial Behavior: Teach and encourage your child to create simple businesses or ventures. Entrepreneurial activities allow your kids to explore their interests, develop problem-solving skills, and learn about supply, demand and pricing. Maybe it is organizing a lemonade stand, selling homemade crafts or providing services like dog walking or lawn mowing in the neighborhood. Teaching your child about how to earn money is an ongoing process. Use age-appropriate language and activities, expect and allow mistakes, and use those moments as learning opportunities.

2. ENJOY AND SPEND

Most people tend to focus on the spending aspect of the dollar. The driving questions are: "What can I buy? What will people think of me if I have this outfit or drive this car?" These questions come from our culture of reinforcement and immediate gratification.

When it comes to spending, there are two categories: Is it a need or a want? Set a precedent for always asking: "Do you *need* that, or do you *want* that?"

If it's a want and not a need, it doesn't mean an automatic *no* —it might be just "not right now." Looking at wants and needs is also an opportunity to teach your child how to save up money for higher ticket items.

One well-known story revolves around two wolves. According to legend, a wise grandfather uses the metaphor of two wolves, one representing evil and the other good, engaged in an internal battle. Curiously, the grandson inquires about the outcome, asking, "Which wolf will win?" The grandfather replies, "The one you feed."

The same concept applies to decision-making when it comes to money. It is similar to the well-known saying that if you fail to establish control over your dog from the beginning, it will eventually dominate you. You wouldn't want your money (or your dog) to have control over you.

The mistake that people make is they spend 100% of every dollar they make and ignore the other four faces of the dollar which is about creating balance between today and tomorrow.

3. SAVE

People often save money so they can spend it on themselves in the future, or have a "rainy day" fund for future emergencies. People also save up for investments or charitable giving. For kids, it might be saving for a new toy or game.

The key to getting your kids hooked on saving is to make conversations about saving engaging and educational. Teaching them about the importance of saving early on is a valuable life skill they will carry throughout their lives.

You can use the following strategies to encourage your kids to save money:

Set Savings Goals: Show your kids that saving is a regular part of life by doing it yourself. Discuss your own saving goals as you help your kids define theirs. Having a clear objective makes saving more tangible and rewarding.

Introduce a Piggy Bank: No matter your child's age, give them a physical place to keep their money. A piggy bank or a clear jar allows them to see their savings grow and provides a tangible representation of the concept.

Match Their Savings: Encourage saving by offering to match a percentage of their savings. This mimics how an employer might match a 401K and reinforces the idea that saving is a positive and rewarding habit.

Open a Savings Account in Their Name: Take them to the bank and explain how a bank account works. Many banks offer special accounts for children with little to no fees.

4. INVEST FOR FUTURE FREEDOM

Investing allows money to grow just like planting seeds in a garden. Investing is a starting point, and the goal is to grow something without having to do much. Teaching kids the importance of investing at a young age can set them on a path to financial success and responsibility.

You can begin to teach your child about the concept of investing by looking at businesses that are of interest to them. Start by looking at what products they are using in their everyday lives (such as their cell phone) and ask questions about it:

- Who made your phone?
- How much do they sell it for?
- How many do they sell?
- Do they make money?
- Do they not make money?
- Who owns the company?
- What is their brand about? (Look at Facebook, Instagram, Snapchat, YouTube, TikTok and Google for clues.)

There are all kinds of real-world examples, but make sure the company produces something your kid is interested in. Look at the health of the business as you begin to explore what would make a good investment.

Point out that your kid can view themselves as a kind of "business" as well. The health of their "business" can be determined by how much they earn and how much money is left over.

As you delve deeper into these money conversations, your child will eventually learn concepts like time versus money and wage earner versus owner (more on this in Chapter 7).

Not only can they use their talents to earn money (no matter their age) and learn how to budget, they can also invest in themselves. That includes forming good habits that allows them to plan ahead and invest time and attention into themselves. The following tips are a good way to introduce the concept of investing:

Use Real-life Examples: Share stories or examples of successful investors. Use relatable examples, such as how investing in a favorite toy or game today can lead to more toys or games in the future as they earn money (as long as it's a good investment).

Introduce the Power of Compound Interest: Teach them about the concept of compound interest and how money can grow over time. Use simple illustrations or online tools to demonstrate how investments can help them accumulate wealth.

Make It Simple: Introduce the idea of investing with simple examples. Discuss how buying shares of a company is like owning a small piece of that company. You can use familiar brands or companies that your child recognizes.

Connect Investing to Their Goals: Discuss how investing can help them achieve long-term goals, such as saving for college or buying a car or bike. This can make the idea of investing more meaningful for them.

Invest Gift Money: If your child receives money as a gift for their birthday or holidays, consider encouraging them to invest a portion of it. By doing so, you are introducing the idea of an investing ratio early on (that part of all earnings should go toward investments, including a retirement account).

Later, they will discover if they make a dollar, a portion of that dollar can go to taxes while another portion can be used for investments. They will soon discover that investing can turn a one-time gift into a growing asset over time.

Think of it like growing a garden. Planting seeds, watering them and patiently waiting for them to grow will eventually yield beautiful flowers, delicious fruits or vegetables.

If it isn't feasible to plant a garden with your child, simply have them plant a few seeds in a container and take care of the plant. By doing so, your child will understand the time and effort required to nurture something and not see the rewards until later.

Remember to keep the discussions age-appropriate, engage their curiosity and make learning about investing a positive and enjoyable experience.

Not only can investing be fun, but it can also be a great way to have a positive impact on society. For example, recently NBA Star Giannis Antetokounmpo teamed up with Calamos Investments to offer investors a sustainable investment product that focuses on performance—striving to beat the S&P 500 with lower risk over the long term—through companies and investment funds that deliver positive societal impacts.[1]

5. GIVE AND SHARE

When you give something away, you demonstrate an abundance mindset. In contrast, a scarcity mindset is about not having enough. Someone with a scarcity mindset might say, "I can't donate my money to a charity because I don't have enough myself." Those with an abundance mindset view things differently, knowing that what they give, they will get back—perhaps even tenfold.

I firmly believe that giving naturally creates an abundance mindset, and that the money donated will come back to you in different ways and at different times. You can teach your child the value of giving by doing the following:

Lead by Example: Demonstrate the importance of giving by making charitable donations yourself. Share your own experiences with your children, explaining why you choose to support certain causes.

Discuss the Impact of Charitable Giving: Talk to your kids about the positive impact charitable donations can have on people and communities. Share stories or videos that show how donations make a difference in the lives of others.

Involve Them in the Decision-making Process: Let your children have a say in what charities or causes to support by sharing their preferences. This can make the experience more meaningful for them.

Connect Giving to Values: Help your kids identify their values and connect those values to charitable causes. Use online resources or visit local organizations with your children to research and learn more about different charities that align with their values.

Create a Giving Jar: Encourage your children to contribute a portion of their allowance or money they earn from chores to the giving jar. Periodically, as a family, decide where to donate the collected funds.

Use Special Occasions: Encourage charitable giving as part of special occasions. For birthdays or holidays, suggest that your child consider donating a portion of their gift money to a charity of their choice.

Talk About Different Forms of Giving: Help your children understand that giving doesn't always involve money. They can donate their time, talents or items to those in need. You can also volunteer as a family, which reinforces the idea that giving goes beyond just giving money away.

As you help your kids develop good money habits that stick, recognize how consistent *little* money conversations can make a *big* difference in their future. Teaching our kids about financial literacy is great, but it does no good if we don't take the time to show them how to be consistent about building good money habits.

WHAT'S THE HARDEST CONCEPT FOR KIDS TO GRASP WHEN IT COMES TO MONEY?

That's easy. The idea that you can't spend everything that you make! This is fundamental and the key takeaway of this chapter. The moment you internalize that as you earn, you spend some of it, save some of it, invest some of it and give some of it away, you will achieve balance.

Think of it like telling your child, "You can have some ice cream, but ice cream can't be the only thing you eat." You have to take things in proportion. Consistently practicing this approach will build a strong foundation. Many people never achieve financial stability because they spend everything they make. Nobody took the time to teach them anything different.

By saving and investing, you create what is called free cash flow—what's left over after spending. Teaching this concept to your child gives them a significant advantage over others. This is foundational and, admittedly, difficult, but continually talk about free cash flow with your kids. It's how people measure their financial health and how companies measure their performance. It's a universal concept in the economic world.

Start encouraging your kids to think of their lives as a business. A company with no free cash flow will eventually go out of business.

I'd like to close this chapter with a quote by F.M. Lawrence: "People do not decide their futures—they decide their habits and their habits decide their futures."

Remember this consistency is more important than execution. With consistency, execution will always improve but without consistency, execution dies.

KEY TAKEAWAYS

- The "Five Faces of the Dollar" concept teaches kids about the multifaceted nature of money, covering earning, spending, saving, investing and giving. It emphasizes that money has more potential than just purchasing power.
- Don't spend 100% of earnings, but rather distribute money across the five "faces" to create balance between present needs and future goals.
- Embrace an abundance mindset, particularly through giving and sharing, which can lead to greater financial and personal growth.
- Consistent practice of good money habits is more crucial than perfect execution. Habits, not single decisions, shape our financial future.

CHAPTER 7
BREAK THE CHAINS OF
THE PAST

"Dream big, start small, but most of all, start."
—Simon Sinek

LESSON: NOW IS THE TIME TO BREAK THE CHAINS THAT BIND YOU TO the past and forge a new pathway of learning with your child so they can experience a different way of being.

When it comes to money, our past operates much like a computer program running silently in the background. We often don't realize it's there, influencing us in subtle and powerful ways. If your parents were frugal, you might find yourself pinching pennies, feeling an unconscious need to "save for a rainy day." If they were spenders, you might be quick to swipe your card, echoing the habits you witnessed growing up.

Entrepreneurial parents may pass on a knack for taking risks, building businesses, or constantly looking for new opportunities. And if money was always a point of stress or complaint ("There's never enough!"), it's likely that narrative now shapes your financial mindset too.

The way we think about and handle money is largely molded by early experiences, a default mode we often carry into adulthood. Just like a software program, these beliefs can run unnoticed, influencing everything from how we spend, save, invest and even dream about the future.

But what happens when those beliefs are limited? What happens when they create patterns that no longer serve us or align with the financial future we want to build? If we don't actively confront them, our past can too easily become our future simply because that's what we know—even if it isn't what's best for us.

What's the impact of early money programming?

If you grew up in a household where money was tight, you may have internalized the belief that financial scarcity is inevitable. This scarcity mindset becomes the lens through which you view every financial decision. You may avoid taking risks, always holding onto what you have, afraid that spending or investing could bring disaster. In contrast, if money seemed to flow freely in your childhood, the idea of budgeting might feel too restrictive. Maybe you're prone to living in the moment, confident that somehow, there will always be enough.

Your past experiences, especially those formed during your childhood, shape your understanding of what money represents. For example:

Frugality: If your parents stressed the importance of saving every penny, you may feel a constant need to save, sometimes to the detriment of enjoying your life or taking calculated risks. You may even find it difficult to spend money on experiences or material things, feeling guilt or anxiety every time you part with a dollar.

Spending: If your childhood was marked by excess, or if your parents had the habit of spending beyond their means, you might follow a similar path. Without even realizing it, you might adopt the same patterns of living paycheck to paycheck, repeating the same cycle you saw growing up.

Entrepreneurship: If your parents ran a business, or pursued entrepreneurial ventures, you might naturally gravitate toward creating your own income streams. You may feel more comfortable with risk and uncertainty because that was normalized for you. On the flip side, if your parents avoided risk at all costs, you might struggle with the idea of venturing into entrepreneurship or even investing, fearing the unknown.

Scarcity Mindset: If money was a source of stress and anxiety in your home, you might have inherited the belief that there's never enough, even when your financial situation changes in a positive way. This belief can lead to a hoarding mentality, where no amount of money or savings ever feels like it's enough.

While none of these behaviors are good or bad, it's the unconscious nature of them that poses a problem. Without having self-awareness, these ingrained beliefs will continue to shape your financial future, and quite possibly, the future of your children too.

WHY ARE THE FINANCIAL HABITS WE LEARN AS KIDS SO HARD TO BREAK AS ADULTS?

Most of us don't realize just how much we've absorbed from our parents' attitudes and behaviors about money. It's not just being told to save or hearing complaints about bills—it's the subtle cues we internalize over years of watching how money was handled in the household we grew up in.

If your parents argued about money, you may unconsciously associate financial discussions with tension and conflict. You might avoid talking about finances with your spouse or partner, thinking that money conversations inevitably lead to arguments. If money was never discussed in your household, you might struggle to engage in meaningful financial planning because it feels uncomfortable or foreign.

Even the way your parents framed wealth can influence you. If wealth was seen as something unattainable or only for "other people," you may harbor beliefs that financial success is out of reach for you, too. On the other hand, if wealth was considered a symbol of success and power, you might feel pressure to chase certain financial milestones, even if they don't align with your personal values or goals.

These "invisible chains" bind us to behaviors that no longer serve us, yet they persist in the background, guiding our decisions without us fully realizing it. And without taking the time to examine where these beliefs come from, we often repeat them in our own lives while passing them down to our kids.

HOW DO WE BREAK FREE FROM THESE INVISIBLE CHAINS?

To break the chains of the past, we must do the difficult work of self-examination. What does that mean? It requires taking a full inventory of your financial history—how you were raised, what you learned and how those lessons continue to influence you today. This isn't about blaming your parents; it's about gaining clarity so you can consciously decide which beliefs to keep and which to release.

Start by asking yourself some probing questions:

- What was money like in my home growing up?
- How did my parents handle finances, and how did that affect me?
- What stories were told about money in my family? Were they positive or negative?
- Was money a source of stress, comfort, control, or something else?

- How did my parents react to financial challenges? Was there panic, anxiety or calm problem-solving?
- How were purchases handled? Was spending a guilt-ridden activity or was it celebrated without any boundaries?
- Did my family place value on saving or investing for the future?
- What messages, spoken or unspoken, shaped my attitudes toward money?
- Are my current financial behaviors and decisions a reflection of my upbringing?
- What patterns do I see in my spending, saving or investing that might not align with the future I want to build?
- Do I feel anxious, guilty, or stressed when making financial decisions, and where might those feelings come from?

Once you have an inventory, it's time to analyze what works for you and what doesn't. If you are frugal, you may discover your frugality is rooted more in fear than in wisdom. Or maybe your aversion to budgeting comes from a false sense of security. The idea is not to erase everything but to intentionally decide what stays and what needs to go.

If you grew up in a family where money was scarce and your parents constantly worried about bills and lived paycheck to paycheck, you may be internalizing a deep fear of financial instability. As an adult, you might overcompensate by hoarding money, being overly conservative with investments or avoiding growth opportunities because you're terrified of losing what you have.

On the flip side, someone who grew up in a household of spenders might have never learned the discipline of saving. Even if they earn a good income, they may struggle to live within their means.

These financial habits, beliefs, and behaviors aren't choices—they're defaults. But they don't have to be.

WHAT'S THE BEST WAY TO BUILD A NEW MINDSET AROUND MONEY?

By confronting your limiting beliefs, you open the door to a world of possibility—not just for you, but for your children and future generations as well. Take the following steps to make lasting change:

Acknowledge and Release Limiting Beliefs: Identify the beliefs that have held you back—whether they stem from fear, scarcity, or inherited ideas about money. Recognize they are just beliefs, not facts. For example, if you grew up thinking *money is always tight*, challenge that belief by recognizing that financial abundance is possible through informed decision-making and disciplined habits.

Adopt a Growth Mindset: Replace limiting beliefs with an abundance mindset. This means shifting from thinking *there's never enough* to *there's always more to learn, earn and create*. A growth mindset around money opens you up to new opportunities—from investing to entrepreneurship—and fosters resilience in the face of financial challenges. It's about viewing money not as something scarce and finite but as a tool for creating new possibilities.

Create New Financial Habits: If you want to shift from a scarcity mentality to one of abundance, start with forming new routines like tracking your spending, setting intentional goals and celebrating your financial wins, no matter how small. For example, if you've always avoided budgeting because it feels restrictive, try reframing it as a tool for empowerment and control, allowing you to direct your money toward what truly matters.

Teach Your Children: Break the cycle for the next generation. The beliefs you challenge today will influence the financial programming of your children tomorrow. Be transparent about money with them. Share your journey and empower them with the knowledge that they can shape their own financial future. Rather than passing down limiting beliefs about money, encourage them to embrace an abundance mindset where they view money as a tool for growth and possibility.

––––––

KEY TAKEAWAYS

- Digging into your past and analyzing your deeply ingrained habits and mindsets will make you uncomfortable. But, the alternative is worse. If you don't take these steps, your past will become your child's future.
- The reward for confronting your financial programming is financially empowering your kids.
- As a parent, you get to choose to let the old program keep running or rewrite it to set a new course for you and your child's financial future.

CHAPTER 8
FOMO AND ENVY ARE TODAY'S CANCER

"Giving in to the fear of missing out (FOMO) can lead you to miss out on something even greater: the life that you truly desire."
—Aili Kuutan

LESSON: FOMO AND ENVY ARE NOTHING NEW, BUT THEY ARE NOW a modern epidemic because of social media. With social media, outside validation becomes the goal, not internal self worth.

Envy—especially in today's social media-driven world—is like a quiet, persistent poison that erodes our sense of self-worth. Social media platforms are designed to show us the best, most glamorous moments of others' lives—carefully curated snapshots of success, beauty and happiness. This constant stream of perfection can make it seem as though everyone else is living a better, more fulfilling life.

Over time, it can create a false narrative in our minds: if they are doing so well, what does that say about me? Am I falling behind? This mindset leads us down a dangerous path where someone else's success feels like a personal failure, feeding the belief that we are "less than."

The deeper danger lies in the fact that these comparisons are not real. We're not seeing the whole picture: the struggles, the insecurities, the everyday challenges that everyone faces. We are comparing our real, unfiltered lives to someone else's highlights. Yet, in our pursuit of living up to these unattainable images, we lose sight of what truly matters: our own progress and happiness.

The critical message we need to instill in our children is that their worth is not determined by how they measure up to others, especially those on social media. The real competition is not external; it's internal. Are they becoming better versions of themselves? Are they making progress toward their own goals, no matter how small?

True growth and personal development happen through small, incremental steps over time. Each of these steps builds on the last, leading to significant results over the long term, but only when we measure ourselves against our own potential and progress. Teaching our children to focus on their own journey will shield them from the constant frustration and dissatisfaction that come from trying to keep up with an unrealistic ideal.

The game of comparing ourselves to others is unwinnable because there will always be someone who appears to have more. Instead, when we orient our kids to compete only against their past selves, we empower them to find genuine fulfillment and develop resilience. They'll learn that success is not about instant results or beating someone else—it's about steady, meaningful progress that aligns with their own values and aspirations. This mindset leads to a life filled with contentment, growth and true achievement, rather than one shadowed by constant feelings of inadequacy.

You might be familiar with the popular saying, "keeping up with the Joneses," which is about a family obsessed with making sure they have more and better possessions than their neighbors. Thanks to social media, we now have to "keep up with the Instagrammers," where people spend money to pursue lifestyles they can't afford in order to one-up influencers on social media platforms. Now, the neighborhood of the Joneses has expanded to the digital world where FOMO has become an obsession.

SO HOW DOES FOMO WORK AND IS IT HARMFUL?

In today's hyper-connected world, the fear of missing out—commonly known as FOMO—has become a pervasive psychological phenomenon. Stemming from a deep-seated desire to stay connected and not miss out on rewarding experiences, FOMO can significantly distort our perception of what we truly need to be doing to lead a fulfilling life.

Besides the perception of missing out, there's a compulsion to maintain these social connections as it is tied to the need to belong and form strong, stable interpersonal relationships.[1] Research shows that FOMO is linked to lack of sleep, reduced life competency, emotional tension, negative effects on physical well-being, anxiety and a lack of emotional control.[2]

Social media exacerbates FOMO by providing a constant stream of other people's curated highlights, making it difficult to resist the urge to compare ourselves to others.

FOMO compels us to measure our worth not by our own progress but by the milestones and possessions of those around us. This relentless comparison creates a toxic cycle where we are perpetually dissatisfied, regardless of our actual achievements.

The danger lies in the fact that there will always be someone who has more, does more or appears to be happier, leading to a never-ending chase for an elusive sense of contentment.

WHY IS THE COMPARISON TRAP SO TEMPTING AND HOW DO YOU GET OUT OF IT?

Social media screams, "My life is great. Yours sucks. You need to be more like me." Money won't make you happy. If you're seeking external validation from others, you're never going to be rich enough. There's always somebody who will have more money than you.

You need to be the one challenging yourself. It's you against you, not you against the internet. That's what you want to teach your kids. The disease of FOMO is a loser's game. That's why celebrities commit suicide and why lottery winners are broke after a few years. They are miserable despite the fame and money.

To help get away from the trappings of social media where somebody always has a better life than you, I've embraced a different approach when it comes to comparing myself to others. Dan Sullivan and Dr. Benjamin Hardy refer to it in their book, *The Gap and The Gain,* where they stay out of "the gap" and focus on "the gain."

"The gap" refers to the tendency to focus on the distance between where you are and where you want to be, or between yourself and others who seem more successful than you. When you're in "the gap," you're constantly comparing your current situation to an ideal or to someone else's achievements, often leading to feelings of inadequacy, frustration or dissatisfaction.

When comparing yourself to others, with "gap" thinking you focus on how far ahead others are, what they have that you don't or how much more successful they seem. This often leads to negative emotions and can be demotivating.

"The gain" represents the progress you've made from where you started to where you are now. It's about acknowledging and appreciating the improvements, growth and achievements you've accomplished over time.

When comparing yourself to others, with "gain" thinking you recognize your own progress, celebrate your achievements and use others' success as inspiration rather than a source of discouragement. This approach tends to be more motivating and positive.

For example, John falls into the comparison trap where he's focused on "the gap." He works hard to afford a beautiful house.

He takes pride in his home, finding joy in its comfort and beauty. However, his neighbor, Mike, recently bought a boat. Suddenly, John isn't so satisfied with his house as he begins to envy Mike's new boat.

Another neighbor, Sarah, not only has a boat but also a private plane. John's envy grows. Meanwhile, his house seems smaller and less significant in comparison to hers. Down the street, there's Peter, who has an even bigger boat than Mike and Sarah. John feels increasingly inadequate, his initial happiness now overshadowed by a constant longing for what he doesn't have.

FOMO happens. Instead of appreciating what we have achieved, we become fixated on the possessions of others. As a result, we are never satisfied.

FOMO is like a cancer in today's society, eroding our ability to find joy in our own lives. It creates a culture of perpetual dissatisfaction, where happiness is always contingent on acquiring the next big thing or reaching the next milestone.

This mindset is not only exhausting but also fundamentally flawed. Happiness can't be attained through comparison and competition. True contentment arises from within, from recognizing and valuing our unique journeys and accomplishments and also measuring progress rather than the destination.

Social media fuels this societal cancer, presenting a distorted reality where everyone appears to be thriving more than we are. It bombards us with images of others' successes, travels and possessions, making it difficult to resist the urge to compare and feel inadequate. This constant comparison erodes our self-esteem and blinds us to our own progress and achievements.

WHAT ARE SOME OTHER STRATEGIES TO AVOID FOMO?

To shift from "the gap" to "the gain," John could start by acknowledging the hard work and dedication it took to buy his house. Instead of envying his neighbors' boats and planes, he could focus on what brings him joy and fulfillment. FOMO can distort our perception of what we need to be happy. It drives us to compare ourselves against others, creating a cycle of perpetual dissatisfaction.

John might take up gardening, a hobby he has always enjoyed, and find contentment in the beauty he creates in his backyard. By appreciating his own accomplishments and pursuing activities that genuinely make him happy, John can break free from the grip of FOMO.

Happiness comes from within, and it is only by appreciating our own achievements and pursuing what genuinely fulfills us that we can find true contentment. In a world where there will always be someone with more, the key to happiness lies in recognizing that we are enough just as we are.

WHAT CAN PARENTS DO TO HELP THEIR KIDS FOCUS ON "THE GAIN"?

Here are some ways to promote embracing progress against yourself rather than against others:

Emphasize Personal Growth Over External Goals: Teach your kids that their primary competition is themselves. Encourage them to focus on their own progress and personal achievements instead of constantly comparing themselves to others.

Celebrate Effort and Progress: Highlight and praise the effort and progress your kids make, regardless of the outcome. Celebrate the small steps and incremental improvements they achieve.

Model Healthy Goal-Setting: Show them how to set realistic and meaningful goals that are based on their values and interests, rather than societal pressures or external validation. Share your own experiences of setting and achieving personal goals to provide relatable examples.

Teach the Value of Intrinsic Rewards: Help your kids understand that true satisfaction and happiness come from within. Emphasize the importance of mastering new skills, overcoming challenges, and staying true to their values.

Encourage Mindfulness and Gratitude: Encourage your kids to appreciate the present moment and reflect on their daily accomplishments and express gratitude for their progress and the support they receive. This practice can help them stay grounded and focused on their own personal journey.

Provide Perspective on Materialism: Explain that while new clothes, cars or gadgets can provide temporary happiness, true contentment comes from personal growth and meaningful relationships. Share examples from your own life where material possessions lost their appeal over time.

Create a Supportive Environment: Encourage your kids to take risks, try new things and learn from their experiences without fear of judgment or punishment. This supportive atmosphere can help them develop resilience and a growth mindset.

Model Resilience and Adaptability: Show your children how to handle setbacks and failures with resilience and adaptability. Share your own stories of overcoming obstacles and adapting to change. Demonstrating these traits helps them understand that setbacks are opportunities for growth and learning, not reasons to give up.

Focus on the Long-Term: Reinforce the idea that personal development is a lifelong journey. Remind your children that consistent effort and self-improvement over time yield significant results. Whether they aspire to be athletes, programmers, artists, or leaders, their journey is unique and should be appreciated for its own merits.

Promote Self-Reflection: Encourage your kids to regularly reflect on their goals, values and progress. They can do this through journals or by asking them guided reflection questions to help them articulate their thoughts and feelings.

Teach the Importance of Internal Fulfillment: True happiness comes from within and is based on internal values and goals. It's the internal struggle and the journey towards self-improvement that bring lasting fulfillment.

Reframe Challenges as Opportunities: Help your kids see challenges and failures as opportunities to learn and grow. This reframing can reduce the fear of failure and encourage a mindset of continuous improvement.

Highlight the Long-Term Benefits of Self-Improvement: Share the long-term benefits of consistently striving to be a better version of oneself. Explain that this approach can lead to significant achievements over time, whether it's becoming an Olympic athlete, a successful programmer or a leader in their field.

Foster Independence and Self-Reliance: Encourage your kids to take ownership of their goals and achievements.

When you allow your kids to make their own decisions and learn from their experiences, this helps them build confidence in their abilities and understand that their success is a result of their own efforts.

Be Patient and Consistent: Personal growth and development take time. Be patient and consistent in your support and encouragement. Celebrate small victories and progress along the way, and remind your kids that the journey is just as important as the destination.

As you help your kids understand that becoming a better version of themselves over time leads to tremendous results, you help them build resilience, self-confidence and a sense of purpose. This mindset not only helps them avoid the pitfalls of FOMO but also equips them with the tools to navigate life's challenges with a positive and growth-oriented attitude.

To better understand how FOMO can impact your life as a parent, ask yourself the following questions:

- Are there any areas in your life where you find yourself obsessed? If so, is there an unresolved internal need you are trying to fill?
- What about your life and work do you love?
- Do you have a long enough timetable to truly slow down and enjoy being here, or are you trying to quickly get *there*?
- Look at your life right now—what are all the "Gains" you can think of?
- How would your priorities change if you were looking at your long-term goals?

If you don't address FOMO with your kids early on and anchor them to family values, they'll be on the treadmill of other people's lives, which will never be fulfilling. When you're living somebody else's life, you are not living your own. Core values need to be instilled by parents, not "influencers."

––––––

KEY TAKEAWAYS

- Social media creates FOMO by providing a constant stream of other people's curated highlights, making it difficult to resist the urge to compare ourselves to others.
- Success should be measured by comparing ourselves to what we've done in the past rather than comparing ourselves to others. It's about progress and the consistent pursuit of learning and improvement that gives us self satisfaction.
- Download my Progress Map at www.401kid. education.

CHAPTER 9
TAKE RISKS: RAISE KIDS THAT AREN'T AFRAID TO TRY

"We take risks all the time, we talk about failure. We need big failures in order to move the needle."
—Jeff Bezos

LESSON: AS YOUR KIDS FACE CHALLENGES AND FAILURES, DON'T ROB them of these experiences. Learn to let them fail. Innovation generally comes from those that aren't conformists.

A friend of mine is a swim instructor. Some of the younger kids, around age two, are terrified when they come to their first lesson. It's common for kids that age to kick and scream to show their resistance to getting into the water.

My friend has observed how the parents who are nervous about their kids swimming transmit that fear to their children. When parents cave and let their child skip swim lessons because they are afraid, they are actually setting the precedent for future behaviors.

Those will be the kids who wear "floaties" at the pool when they are older and get teased because they don't know how to swim. When you go through life with "floaties" on, you compromise your confidence in everything you do.

In contrast, if the parents are excited about their child

learning to swim and ignore the temper tantrum, the child is able to push past the fear and get in the water and learn to swim.

The story shows how not confronting fear limits us. If we play it safe, we don't grow and get the opportunity to create value out in the world. If we venture out, we gain self-esteem. We grow when we have the courage to try new things. Just ask Jeff Bezos.

Jeff Bezos recognized early on that most large companies embrace the concept of invention but aren't willing to endure failed attempts to get there. Amazon's business philosophy is centered on creating value for customers, taking a long-term approach, embracing innovation and taking risks. He viewed taking chances and failure as simply part of doing business.

Bezos shared his thoughts about the importance of risk-taking in an interview: "When you think about the things that you will regret when you're 80, they're almost always the things that you did not do. They're acts of omission. Very rarely are you going to regret something that you did that failed and didn't work."[1]

That line of thinking paid off for Bezos, as his net worth in 2024 is nearly $180 billion. His business philosophy ties in with this chapter's theme of raising kids that aren't afraid to try *and* fail.

By showing your kids that they can be thoughtful about the risks they take, they learn that they don't need guaranteed success to try. After all, trying is a huge part of their growth.

Bezos saw an opportunity to create value for people, and doing so took a risk. Similarly, helping your kids stay committed to the value they can create for others, even in the face of uncertainty, fosters resilience and a willingness to persevere. This resilience is what propels them forward, even when they encounter setbacks or failures.

Just as Bezos persisted through challenges to build Amazon into the behemoth it is today, instilling in your children the importance of staying true to their values and goals can empower them to overcome obstacles and achieve their dreams.

By encouraging them to embrace failure as a natural part of the learning process, you equip them with the mindset needed to navigate life's ups and downs with confidence and determination.

As parents, it's natural to want our children to be confident, adaptable and ready to take on any challenge that comes their way. We may fantasize about a future where our kids fearlessly pursue their dreams despite the obstacles they encounter. We want to raise courageous kids. But this courage needs nurturing.

HOW CAN YOU AND WHY SHOULD YOU CULTIVATE THIS KIND OF COURAGE IN YOUR KID?

It all comes down to embracing the concept of risk-taking. By encouraging our kids to embrace risks, we empower them to develop essential skills that will serve them throughout their lives.

Taking risks fuels creativity, nurtures problem-solving abilities, and fosters adaptability. When kids aren't afraid to try *and* fail, they can uncover their true potential.

By teaching our kids to be comfortable with taking risks, we equip them with the tools they need to navigate through life's uncertainties, grasp new opportunities and make a lasting impact. It is only by stepping outside their comfort zones that our kids can courageously explore their talents, passions and capabilities.

Encouraging them to take calculated risks helps them build resilience and confidence. Persevering in the face of adversity allows them to seize opportunities others may miss.

In some cultures, particularly in Southeast Asia, it was once common practice to tether young elephants with heavy chains attached to strong stakes driven deep into the ground. The young elephants would struggle against the chains, trying to break free, but because they were not yet strong enough, they would eventually give up.

As these elephants grew older and stronger, their handlers would replace the heavy chains with lighter ones and replace the strong stakes with simple wooden stakes. Despite being fully capable of breaking free, the adult elephants had already learned from their past experiences that they were unable to escape the restraints.

As a result, even though the chains were no longer strong enough to hold them, the adult elephants would still remain tethered to the stakes, never attempting to break free. Their belief system had been shaped by their previous experiences.

The elephant story is a perfect illustration of how limiting beliefs formed early in life can continue to hold people back, even when the circumstances that originally created those beliefs are no longer relevant or true. This relates to money too.

You want to teach your kids to challenge and overcome limiting beliefs about themselves that might prevent them from pursuing opportunities that create value for others and potentially lucrative income for themselves. Teaching kids how to take risks is an essential part of their development.

WHAT'S THE BEST WAY TO GIVE KIDS A GROWTH MINDSET TO OVERCOME THEIR LIMITING BELIEFS?

When kids face failure, make mistakes or experience the disappointment of losing a game, our response can shape their attitudes toward risk-taking and resilience. Encouragement during these challenging moments can foster a growth mindset, while criticism can lead to fear of failure and hinder their willingness to try new things.

When children are learning—whether it's a new sport, a musical instrument or a challenging class in school—there's a lot of trial and error involved. If we give predominantly negative feedback to their inevitable setbacks, it can discourage them from pushing their boundaries.

When we focus on current failures, we miss the bigger picture. For instance, a pilot may veer off course multiple times during a flight but ultimately land safely. If we were to focus only on the moments when things didn't go perfectly, we might overlook the skill and determination that led to a successful landing. The same concept applies to our kids. They need to understand that mistakes are a part of the journey toward achieving great things.

Kids are often their own harshest critics. If they consistently hear negative feedback from us, it can reinforce their self-doubt. Instead of nurturing their confidence and resilience, we risk instilling a fear of failure that can persist well into adulthood.

By honing in on the positive outcomes of their efforts, we can help our kids recognize the value of perseverance. Celebrating their attempts, regardless of the outcome, teaches them that effort is what counts. Encouragement can take many forms— verbal praise, acknowledgment of their hard work or simply being present and supportive during tough times. It's about creating an environment where your kids feel safe to take risks and understand that making mistakes is a natural part of learning.

By focusing on their growth, we help them become more resilient and a willingness to tackle new challenges with confidence. As parents, we can empower our kids to take risks, learn from their experiences, and be unafraid to pursue their passions.

Sara Blakely, creator of Spanx, shared:

When I was riding my bike with one of my best friends at age 16, she was run over by a car and was killed in front of me. A few months later, my dad left home and my parents separated and ultimately divorced. When my dad moved out, he came into my bedroom and handed me a cassette tape series called *How to Be a No Limit Person* by Wayne Dyer. And he said, 'Sweetie, I wish I discovered this at your age instead of the age of 40.' And then he moved out. And so I started listening to *How to Be a No Limit Person* which was talking about visualization, the law of attraction, not caring what other people think about you and not being consumed by the fear of failure. And the clouds parted for me. I thought I spent a lot of time being taught *what* to think but nobody is teaching me *how* to think. And at age 16 that was so incredibly important. It totally changed my mindset.

The information she received at age 16 ultimately was what gave her the courage to take the risks and become an entrepreneur.

According to Elon Musk:

If you punish people too much for failure then they will respond accordingly and the innovation you get will be very incrementalist. Nobody is going to try anything bold for fear of getting fired or being punished in some way. The risk/reward must be balanced and favor taking bold moves otherwise it will not happen.

WHEN YOU TALK ABOUT RISK, DOES THAT MEAN ENDORSING RISKY BEHAVIOR?

Risky behavior can have both positive and negative consequences. Generally, society tends to place more emphasis on caution, stability and conformity rather than risk-taking. It's rooted in the notion that risks are inherently dangerous and should be avoided to ensure safety and well-being.

Negatively perceived behaviors like gambling, substance abuse or reckless driving often involve a higher likelihood of negative outcomes. Undesirable actions tend to capture more news headlines than "feel good" stories, reinforcing the idea that risk is primarily associated with negative behaviors.

However, risk-taking isn't inherently a bad thing. Taking calculated risks such as starting a business, embracing opportunities for growth or exploring new ventures can pave the way for personal development, achievement and groundbreaking ideas. I advocate encouraging the positive aspects of risk-taking while promoting responsible decision-making. You can do this by:

Defining Risk and Reward: Help your kids understand that risk is related to the possibility of losing something, while reward refers to the benefit that can be gained from taking a certain action.

Evaluating Potential Outcomes: Encourage your kids to evaluate potential outcomes before making decisions. Help your kids consider both the positive and negative consequences of a particular action. Have conversations about how the level of risk is associated with the potential rewards. Maybe it's trying out for the soccer team for the first time. What are the risks of courageously stepping out of their comfort zones to try something new, even though they know they're not going to be immediately successful? While there will be uncertainty and fear, these experiences are integral to personal growth and resilience.

Assessing Personal Values: Help your child understand that risk and reward can be subjective and differ from person to person. Encourage them to consider their own values, goals and priorities when assessing the potential risks and rewards of a situation.

Starting Small and Gradually Increasing Challenges:
Begin by introducing low-risk situations to your child and gradually increase the complexity of the scenarios. This allows them to gain experience and develop their decision-making skills over time.

Encouraging Learning from Mistakes: Mistakes are valuable opportunities for learning. Encourage your child to reflect on past decisions, both successful and unsuccessful, and identify the lessons they can draw from them. Help them understand that taking calculated risks and experiencing setbacks are part of the learning process.

As a parent, you'll be providing your kids with guidance and support on this risk-taking adventure we call life. You will be teaching your kid how to navigate risk in their everyday lives.

By taking risks, they can soar to new heights and unlock their full potential. In contrast, if they constantly play it safe and remain confined within the walls of their comfort zone, it will halt their growth and hinder their progress. This approach indirectly teaches our kids to rely heavily on others and shy away from facing challenges.

HOW CAN RISK-TAKING EQUIP YOUR KID TO COPE WITH CHALLENGING SITUATIONS?

Successful people constantly push their boundaries and embrace discomfort. They recognize the immense power of taking risks, even if it results in temporary setbacks. Ultimately, it is these courageous ventures that pave the way for groundbreaking achievements.

For kids, embracing discomfort can build their confidence and shape their character. Whether it's mustering up the courage to ask someone to dance, taking a leap of faith and trying out for the baseball team or showcasing their hidden talents on stage during the talent show, these are the experiences that can ignite their potential.

It's about not playing it safe all the time. Pursuing dreams will most likely be tied to a financial cost. You need to invest in yourself and evaluate the costs and benefits. Ultimately, you want to achieve a balance between risk and reward. When you dare to try, you open yourself up to a world of growth, success and fulfillment.

This all goes back to what I shared about The Rules of the Game in Chapter 2. Life is a series of obstacles. It is about over-coming those obstacles and then seeing the reward for doing so.

Failing, getting back up, and trying again and again are key elements of The Rules of the Game. By conquering struggles, not only do we boost our self-esteem, but we also show our worth to others. Failure becomes but a stepping stone toward success.

Just like with money conversations, we need to have regular conversations with our kids to help them understand that failure is simply a natural part of life; it's not a character flaw. History has shown that no extraordinary accomplishments have been achieved without enduring a few setbacks and overcoming obstacles along the way.

WHAT ARE SOME WAYS TO SHOW THE UPSIDE OF FAILURE?

ABC's *Wide World of Sports*, a popular show in the 1970s, had a classic intro where host Jim McKay would say, "Spanning the globe to bring you the constant variety of sports...the thrill of victory...and the agony of defeat...the human drama of athletic competition...This is *ABC's Wide World of Sports!*"

The opening scenes showed a Slovenian ski jumper taking a catastrophic crash during a competition displaying what "agony of defeat" looked like.

Participating in sports provides a platform for kids to experi-ence the exhilaration of winning and the disappointment of losing, just like in *ABC's Wide World of Sports*. These contrasting emotions teach invaluable lessons about perseverance, team-work, and resilience.

By learning from victories and defeats, kids become better equipped to navigate the complexities of life and approach challenges differently. The transformative power of sports extends far beyond the game, offering endless opportunities for personal growth, building relationships and embracing the valuable lessons of risk versus rewards.

Through sports, your child will learn how to look for and accept the inevitable stumbling blocks of life. Resilience is the key to thriving in the face of adversity, challenges, or setbacks. It goes beyond mere survival; it empowers people to adapt, recover and bounce back stronger than ever. You want to teach your kids to be tough and gritty so they grow up to be resilient.

Imagine someone who confidently rises above difficult situations, with their well-being intact and their ability to perform at their best undeterred. Maybe it's the professional boxer in the ring who gets punched in the face but keeps fighting back. That's resilience. By cultivating resilience early on, kids acquire a robust skill set that will serve them well throughout their lives.

As parents, it's natural to have a strong instinct to protect our children. This protective instinct is rooted in the fundamental parental drive to ensure the safety, well-being and flourishing of our offspring.

It's this drive that can sometimes lead parents to make poor decisions, even if they have their kids' best interests at heart. Consider the nationwide college exam cheating scandal — what caused these parents to participate? After pleading guilty, Felicity Huffman stated, "It felt like I had to give my daughter a chance at a future. And so it was sort of like my daughter's future, which meant I had to break the law."

Of course you want to protect them from unnecessary harm. That's why we wear seatbelts when in the car and helmets while riding a bike. However, being overprotective of our kids comes with a cost. We want to teach them to aim higher than we did so they can aspire to be better, but we don't want to do this at the expense of hindering their growth or hurting ourselves.

Every risk taken carries the potential for great reward or significant danger. It is crucial to understand that when taking risks, there's a possibility of looking foolish, as the outcome may not always be favorable. Nevertheless, teaching our children the art of embracing risks and potential failures is vital.

Consider the scenario of a teenager asking someone out on a date. While the risk of rejection exists, it is worth taking because the decision boils down to weighing the potential rewards against the risks involved.

Embrace the power of taking risks, as it is the key to unlocking immense value. It involves a process of trial and error, but those who dare to take risks often create the most valuable outcomes. Instill in your kids that risk-taking is an inevitable part of life.

ARE THERE ANY EXAMPLES OF RISK-TAKING THAT YOUR KID MIGHT APPRECIATE?

Let me start with an example of my dad. When he was 12, he was playing tennis in Golden Gate Park in a pickup game wearing jeans, t-shirt and a wooden racket. Somebody noticed him and said, "Hey, you're pretty good. Why don't you play a tennis tournament this weekend over in Berkeley?"

He ran home and asked his mom for a little bit of money to play in the tournament. She responded, "Oh, no, don't do that. You're just going to get beat and you're going to feel bad." Even today, he recalls this moment as a very significant part of his life.

He somehow got the money and ended up going to the tennis tournament and actually won. And then a man walked up to him and said, "Who are you? And who's your mother? I need her number." He called his mom and said, "Hey, your kid is incredible and we want to sponsor him and give him a free membership to the San Francisco Racquet Club."

In the next tennis tournament, they realized his birth date was wrong so he couldn't play with the 12 year olds anymore. He needed to play with the 15 year olds. He was to play the number one 15 year old kid in the country. He almost beat him.

Despite having a mother who encouraged him to be cautious, my dad ended up getting a scholarship to Notre Dame. He still wonders today how his life would have been different if his parents encouraged him to be more courageous.

He learned to play it safe rather than going for it. After college, he had a chance to go pro. Because the voices of the past preyed upon him, he decided not to try and instead got a job.

Those decisions haunt him today. Parents need to understand that the impact of negative talk continues throughout their child's life well into adulthood. Ask yourself if you are a "play it safe parent" or a" let's try and see what happens parent?"

Another example is the movie *Air: A Story of Greatness*, which captures the essence of courage, risk-taking and belief. The inspiring story follows Nike executive, Sonny Vaccaro (played by Matt Damon), as he fearlessly pursues the opportunity to sign the relatively unknown basketball prodigy, Michael Jordan, to create the iconic Air Jordan shoe line.

This tale unfolds during the 1980s when Nike was the third-ranking athletic shoe company. Vaccaro was willing to put everything on the line to secure Jordan's signature, offering him an unprecedented deal worth $250,000 per year along with a percentage of the profits from the Air Jordan line. At the time, this kind of deal was unheard of.

Despite being perceived as foolish by many, including his boss, Phil Knight, the owner of Nike, Vaccaro's relentless pursuit paid off. Both Jordan and his mother were smart enough to know Jordan's value and fought for it alongside Vaccaro. By doing so, they opened themselves up to immense rewards.

Jordan's values of excellence, authenticity, competitiveness, social impact and cultural significance are woven into the fabric of the Air Jordan brand. These values resonate with consumers and drive demand while contributing to the profitability of the Air Jordan shoe line.

Nearly 40 years later, Nike is the top athletic shoe company, and Michael Jordan earns about $400 million annually from his share of the profits.

Just like with Jordan, at the core of any successful endeavor is value creation. Value can manifest in various forms and perspectives. Raising confident kids who aren't afraid to try and fail will allow them to grasp the concept of owner versus wage earner, which we'll delve into in the next chapter.

Being an owner requires a skill set of taking risks and learning from failure—and the path of being one also provides the biggest opportunity for value creation.

AS A PARENT, HOW DO YOU ENCOURAGE EFFORT, NOT RESULTS IN YOUR KIDS?

Jesse Itzler, entrepreneur, New York Times bestselling author and co-founder of Marquis Jet, says, "Praise the effort, not the results," which resonates with me deeply. I grew up in a family of competitors. My father was a collegiate tennis player, and as a player, I had some pretty big shoes to fill. Most of the time, I didn't measure up to my father's standards, leading to frustration on his part. He felt that I wasn't listening to him. This led to a lot of friction between us. Frustrated, I eventually quit tennis.

When my kids started to play tennis, I vowed I would never be that father who yelled at them for their lack of effort or hustle from the sidelines. However, one day when my daughter was 12, she had a very frustrating match and lost. I felt like she had given up, so in my infinite wisdom, I sat her down and sternly talked to her about effort, her commitment and how I felt she had quit. Her body language—slumped and ashamed—hit me like a ton of bricks. I suddenly realized I was behaving just like my dad. I walked away, deeply disappointed in myself. I had become the very person I vowed never to be.

I soon realized, however, that my daughter hadn't quit; she was frustrated with her performance and struggling to figure things out. Once I understood that, we went to Starbucks, got a Frappuccino, and made a pact: we would focus on effort and let the results take care of themselves. We decided not to get too excited on good days or too disappointed on bad days.

Our mantra became Itzler's words about focusing on effort and process, not results. The results will vary. You can't get too excited when your kids do well or too disappointed when they don't as that's the nature of competition. If you instill an effort-oriented mindset, your kids will continually want to put themselves out there, regardless of wins or losses. As a parent, if you focus on wins and losses, you set your kids up for failure because the times they win will be infrequent.

Consider a tennis tournament: 64 kids start, and there is only one winner. The odds are simply against frequent wins. I have seen many parents destroy their kids' love for the game because of their unrealistic expectations. Instead, develop and encourage a mindset where effort is valued. Our kids will fail or underachieve, so creating an environment where that's okay and they're motivated to keep trying is crucial. Harsh criticism can destroy the amazing dreams your kids have.

Positive praise during difficult times can be incredibly empowering for kids. When they face challenges and don't achieve the desired result, acknowledging their hard work and perseverance can help them build resilience. It teaches them that their value isn't tied to success alone but to their character and determination.

Positive reinforcement helps children develop the confidence to tackle future challenges. It's about building their self-esteem and helping them understand that setbacks are temporary and can be overcome with effort and persistence. By creating an environment where effort is celebrated, we help children become more willing to take risks and explore their potential fully. They learn to see failure not as a defeat but as a stepping stone to success.

———

KEY TAKEAWAYS

- If you don't take chances and fail, you'll never succeed.
- Failing is an opportunity to learn.
- Playing it safe is really risky.
- Playing it risky is really safe.
- Encourage your kids to play bigger than you and get out of their comfort zone.
- Encourage effort, not results.
- Download the risk questionnaire for parents at www.401kid.education.

CHAPTER 10
THINK LIKE AN OWNER

"If you don't build your dream, someone else will hire you to help them build theirs."
—Dhirubhai Ambani

LESSON: WHILE WAGE EARNERS CAN GET RICH OVER TIME, IT'S usually at a slow pace. In contrast, owners have the opportunity to accumulate wealth much faster. Anyone can become an owner. It's a simple formula—the power of one versus the power of many.

The Millionaire Next Door, a popular *New York Times* best-selling book, shows how being disciplined over a long period of time while saving money and working for somebody else allows you to become a millionaire. While that is admirable, this is a very slow approach to wealth that doesn't consider ownership. Fortunately, there is also another path to financial freedom: entrepreneurship.

People talk about the money game a lot, but they don't talk enough about the ownership game. It's possible to create wealth much faster as an owner rather than as an employee. That's why I'm here to advocate for the ownership game.

I first met Paul in a class I was teaching in 2004. He shared with me that after he graduated college, he got a job as an engineer at Intel. His dad, a guy with a steady paycheck, told his son, "You will never have to worry about this company. You can spend the rest of your career here. However, while it will be steady income, it may become boring so if you want to try something different, do it early before you have obligations."

Less than nine months after that conversation with his dad, Paul called him to tell him he quit. He wasn't fulfilled and didn't feel he had any meaningful impact. He answered an ad and went to work for a group of guys who were doing some very innovative things on the Internet. They were all smart and driven, but had no clear idea about the prospects of their business. Paul knew he would have a much more significant role in either the success or failure of this venture. He welcomed the challenge, despite the risks.

Paul's decision to work for this small company wasn't about chasing money, it was about chasing impact and making a meaningful contribution. He understood the value of equity and took the majority of his compensation in company stock. He knew that if things didn't work out, he could always fall back on a stable job at a bigger company.

The story has a happy ending: Paul was employee number 23 at Google, which went on to do amazing things. He was instrumental in creating Gmail and had a direct hand in developing Google AdWords.

Currently, there are 31 million entrepreneurs in the U.S., about 16 percent of the adult workforce. About 55% of adults have started a business at some point and 26% have created two or more businesses.[1] I am one of the entrepreneurs reflected in those statistics.

Growing up , my parents never encouraged me to become an entrepreneur. My dad was much more concerned about receiving a paycheck and putting food on the table than exploring riskier options that could lead him toward the world of entrepreneurship.

All of this is understandable. When you are younger, you have a greater ability to take risks because you have less to lose. When you start a family, you have others depending on the financial outcome of your decisions.

My father had offers to work with startup companies that had advancement and equity opportunities that would have put him on the ownership path. But he chose to stay put in his job with the safety net of a larger organization.

While he was successful in his chosen career, he has told me that he regrets that he never learned how to think like an owner and achieve the wealth he was capable of earning when he was younger.

Actual wealth creation is not born from simple wage earning or trading time for money. When you work for somebody else in a conventional job, you trade time for money. You want your kids to grasp this concept of time versus money early on.

It's something you can teach your toddler. You can reward them for completing a simple task. For example, if they pick up their blocks on the floor and put them away, you could give them more play time as a reward. Essentially, you are teaching them the concept of being a wage earner who trades time for money. (In this case, the money is the additional play time.)

You might think that the topic of being an owner should come up when your kids are old enough to legally work. I'd argue that your kids should be familiar with the concept of business ownership much sooner—it's one of the reasons I'm writing this book. Do you think the wage earner income or the owner income will make you richer faster?

WHAT ARE WAYS TO BECOME AN OWNER WITHOUT STARTING YOUR OWN BUSINESS?

You don't have to be a founder to be an owner. Paul didn't start Google, but he became an owner through his stock options. Another great example is Nvidia Corporation, another technology company like Google. In five years, employees with stock options have seen their nest eggs balloon by as much as 1,200%. Because of stock options, most middle managers can make $1 million a year—or more.

Nvidia's longer-tenured employees are wealthy, not because they are wage earners but because of the company's stock, which provides them ownership. As a wage earner, you're limited in your ability to earn because you're one person doing one thing to earn a wage as opposed to an owner who benefits from the work of many wage earners.

I have had the privilege of teaching families that come into sudden wealth through a course I designed 25 years ago. About 98 percent of the wealthy people who attend my class did not become rich through wages. Unless they work in a highly skilled and compensated field like neurosurgery, they became wealthy because they have some element of ownership.

One of my students, who had $8 million to invest, was an administrative assistant who didn't earn a high salary in that role. However, her boss was a highly successful biotech executive who gave her shares in his startup. She would have never accumulated that kind of wealth if she hadn't had those stock shares and was just a wage earner.

WHAT'S THE DIFFERENCE BETWEEN AN OWNER AND EMPLOYEE MINDSET?

The owner and employee mindsets are two distinct perspectives that are not innate. Indeed, people may adopt new or differing perspectives based on their roles and responsibilities within a business. The following are some critical differences between an owner versus employee mindset:

OWNERSHIP OF RESULTS

Owner Mindset: Owners take full responsibility for the success or failure of the business. They are deeply invested in the outcomes, and are willing to take risks and work harder to achieve their goals.

Employee Mindset: Employees typically focus on fulfilling their job responsibilities and meeting specific performance targets set by their employers. While they contribute to the overall success of the business, they may not feel the same level of personal accountability for outcomes.

DECISION-MAKING

Owner Mindset: Owners have the authority to make strategic decisions that impact the direction and operations of the business. They weigh risks and opportunities carefully and have the autonomy to implement changes as they see fit.

Employee Mindset: Employees follow the direction set by management and adhere to established policies and procedures. While they may have input into decision-making processes, the final authority rests with the business owner or higher-level managers. The power of one is more about the individual employee.

LONG-TERM VISION

Owner Mindset: Owners tend to have a long-term perspective and are focused on building a sustainable and profitable business over time. They invest in strategic planning, innovation and growth opportunities that align with their vision for the future. The power of many is about the overall health of the organization.

Employee Mindset: Employees focus more on short-term goals and meeting immediate objectives within their roles. While they may contribute ideas for improvement, their focus is on fulfilling their described job duties and hitting short-term performance targets.

RISK TOLERANCE

Owner Mindset: Owners are often more comfortable taking risks and making bold decisions to pursue opportunities for growth and innovation. They understand that entrepreneurship involves inherent risks and are willing to accept failures as learning experiences.

Employee Mindset: Employees may have a lower tolerance for risk, as they focus primarily on job security and stability. They may prefer to follow established processes and protocols rather than take risks that could jeopardize their position within the company.

SENSE OF OWNERSHIP

Owner Mindset: Owners are emotionally invested in their business's success and are motivated to go above and beyond to ensure its prosperity.

Employee Mindset: While employees may take pride in their work and contribute to the business' success, their sense of ownership is inherently limited to their specific job responsibilities and tasks.

Both employee and owner mindsets play essential roles in the functioning and success of a business. However, being an owner opens the door to opportunities employees do not typically have.

Some of these opportunities include freedom over your time, no cap on income/earning potential and most importantly creating a business that is fulfilling, and working with like-minded people (because you are in charge of hiring them and creating the culture in which they work.)

As noted, you don't need to be a business founder to experience this kind of freedom. Like my student who is an administrative assistant, you can be an employee as well as an owner. Just think about how many millionaires have been created inside companies through stock and ownership. You don't need to look any further than Meta, Google, Microsoft, Walmart, Amazon or Apple.

SO, HOW DO YOU SPARK YOUR KID'S INTEREST IN BUSINESS OWNERSHIP?

I encourage you to show your kids real life examples of their own ability to be a business owner. This could be as simple as having them mow a neighbor's lawn for $20. Considering the time it took to mow the lawn, have them estimate how many lawns they could mow in a day. Then, take it a step further by having them imagine what it would be like if they had an employee who mowed some of those lawns for them for a wage they paid out while they received 25% of the earnings for each lawn mowed. What would that look and feel like?

When having these conversations, you always want to talk about things that interest your children. Start the conversation by exploring what companies your child is familiar with. You can ask them, "What company do you think is cool?" Then together you can investigate if that company is publicly traded. You might continue the conversation, "Did you know that we may be able to buy part of that company? It would involve investing part of your allowance into that company. We could invest half of your weekly allowance while you keep the rest. I'll also match the same amount of money that you invest. As you earn or lose money on your investment, you'll start to see what it feels like to be an owner of a company."

Letting your kids in on the secret that they could actually be part owner of a company they care about is an opportunity to educate them about owner versus employee mindset. This sets the wheels in motion for entrepreneurship and possibly the path to business ownership.

When your kid invariably resists cleaning their room, ask them to imagine what it would be like to own a cleaning company. They could have the cleaning crew tidy the room while they are free to play with their friends. Sharing this imagined scenario could pique their interest about becoming an owner.

When my daughter was younger, she formed an entrepreneurial mindset early on and was interested in the concept of being an owner. At the time, we lived near a hiking trail. There was not enough parking on the road when it got crowded on the weekends, and we had a dirt lot on our property in front of our home that could accommodate lots of parked cars.

My daughter had an idea to charge $20 per car to park in it, earning $500-$1,000 daily on the weekends. Before we agreed to let her be in charge of the parking lot she envisioned, the deal was she needed to invest half of the money she earned, a deal which she fought me on.

That's when I told her, "Spending, you will always find a way to spend 100 percent of your money." What I meant by that is if you aren't disciplined, you'll find a way to spend all the money you make. It takes discipline to put money aside. This relates to owning your business too. It's not possible to run a business spending 100 percent of what you take in. Businesses have this thing called profit; it's what's left after the expenses. Businesses use this money to reinvest in all kinds of things like products and buildings in order to grow. If you don't I told her if she didn't embrace this kind of mindset, she would never grow.

One particular weekend, my daughter was out of town and one of her friends agreed to work the parking lot for her. In return, she offered to pay her half of the revenue for that weekend. That's when my daughter learned the value and the cost of earning money while somebody else was doing the work. She was having fun out of town while her friend was working and giving her 50 percent of the proceeds while her friend was entitled to her own half of the lot earnings. At age 14, she my daughter felt the power of being an owner. The seed of possibility for entrepreneurship was now planted.

HOW CAN YOU TEACH YOUR KIDS ABOUT OWNERSHIP IF YOU'VE ONLY BEEN A WAGE EARNER?

Even if you've never been an owner, you can have plenty of conversations with your child about your career path which will still encourage them to entrepreneurship. Maybe you have worked for the same company for most of your career or maybe you have had multiple jobs that have taken you on different career paths. Whatever your situation is, be open and honest about your experiences. These are teachable moments and your vulnerability and reflection will only encourage conversation. You can share what you wish you would have done differently or opportunities you missed to become an owner yourself.

Though family dynamics, cultural influences, socioeconomic status, and individual interests and aspirations can affect whether children follow their parents' career paths, parental influence can play a significant role in shaping a child's career choices.

With the knowledge that children often naturally choose their parent's career path, Emilio, a landscaper friend of mine in his late 30s, shared with his son how early on in his career he wished he would have started his own landscaping business. He wasn't able to go down that path because life got busy when he became a husband and father.

Having now spent 20 years as a landscaper working for different landscaping companies, Emilio realizes owning his own landscaping business could have completely changed his economic reality. Emilio's hope in sharing his regrets with his son is that he will consider ownership for himself once he grows up.

———

KEY TAKEAWAYS

- You do not need to be an owner yourself to teach your kids about the power of ownership.
- You have the power to change your kid's financial reality.
- Owner and employee mindsets are two distinct perspectives.
- Download the Owners Workbook for you and your kids at www.401kid.education.

CHAPTER 11
CREATE EXCESS WITH YOUR KIDS

"Discipline is doing what you hate to do, but nonetheless doing it like you love it."
—Mike Tyson

LESSON: EXCESS PROVIDES ACCESS TO OPPORTUNITIES OTHERS CAN only imagine.

If there's one thing you take away from this book, let it be this: instill in your kids the value of self-discipline and delayed gratification. That's where the power lies to create the kind of excess money, which can truly open the doors to financial freedom.

AS YOUR KIDS START EARNING MONEY, HOW DO YOU ENSURE THEY HANG ONTO IT?

Up to this point, this book has been about teaching your kids how to create wealth. Now it's time to take the next step; keeping, preserving and building more wealth.

Shaquille "Shaq" O'Neal has some sage advice regarding achieving financial freedom. O'Neal advises, "It's not about how much you make, it's about how much you keep. Save 75 percent of your earnings and put it away. Use the other 25 percent as you please."

As you've already learned, more money earned doesn't necessarily equal more wealth. Now that we've talked about different ways of creating wealth, we can explore what it takes to preserve that wealth and how the sacrifices your kid makes now will pay dividends down the line.

As a parent, you can have the power to make your kid's financial reality different and better than yours. You can encourage your kids to channel their interests and skills into potential businesses, careers, and investment opportunities. They can then translate their enthusiasm, energy, and strengths into financial success.

Who doesn't want their kid to be financially successful and create more value in this world? This is precisely why you want to have those money conversations when they are young. When kids start forming their money habits early on, they become automatic—just like my friends from Australia who crave Vegemite because they were introduced to it when they were infants.

The longer you wait to have these money conversations, the more difficult it becomes. You want to build a strong foundation early on so that you will not have to compete with "influencers" for your child's respect and attention when they begin to use social media. You might not realize it, but your kids are a lot smarter than you think and can handle these conversations even if you yourself are hesitant to initiate them.

WHY IS CREATING EXCESS MONEY SO HARD?

In today's fast-paced, social media-driven world, the mentality of "I want it *now*" has become pervasive. Social media platforms like Instagram, TikTok, X and others showcase the perfectly curated lives of influencers, fueling a desire for instant gratification and the appearance of perfection. Kids are naturally going to want the latest sneakers, outfit, or the latest everything to make themselves look cool, but you don't want your kids to get on that consumerism treadmill because it never ends.

I know someone who is on that treadmill. At age 13, she is all about the latest trends like Lululemon and Stanley cups. Her parents are buying her $200 bottles of lotion because she sees them trending on TikTok. Is her skin soft? Probably. But, what if her parents bought her a $20 bottle of lotion instead and they agreed as a family to invest the difference into her financial future? Her parents aren't teaching her those values though.

The "filtered life" flaunted by social media influencers can overshadow the value of building financial resilience. The temptation to consume and keep up with the perceived affluence of others online often takes precedence over making the difficult decision to delay gratification and put money aside for the future.

Building excess money means delaying what you want for later. Or better yet, reprioritizing needs and wants. It's making the choice to invest rather than consume. It's the difference between today's pleasures and tomorrow's freedom.

Some social media content creators make over $1 million annually—and there's a reason advertisers are willing to pay that amount of money. Advertisers are savvy and realize that social media influencers have the power to sway their followers' opinions and purchasing decisions. Brands often collaborate with influencers to promote their products or services. Influencers can range from public figures to everyday people who have built a following around a specific passion or interest.

What sets influencers apart is their ability to engage and connect with their audience personally, often leading to high trust and loyalty. That can lead to some dangerous territory. Think about it: Who does your child trust for "advice" online?

WHAT ARE SOME OF THE DANGERS AND GOALS OF SOCIAL MEDIA?

Seeing influencers living their "best life" can create feelings of envy and inadequacy in followers, driving them to spend money they don't have in order to keep up. Followers aren't seeing the whole picture, of course, because influencers use curated depictions in their posts. These posts don't show the full reality of what's going on in influencers' lives, nor do they show the darker side of social media.

According to the CDC, suicide is the second-leading cause of death in children and young adults ages 10 to 24.[1] Excessive use of social media can cause cyberbullying, social comparison, social isolation and the spreading of harmful content. All of this can contribute to depression, low self-esteem and suicidal ideation, particularly among youth and young adults.

In January 2024, during a landmark hearing, the Senate Judiciary Committee pressed five big tech CEOs of Discord, Meta, Snap, TikTok and X on failures to protect kids from online exploitation. At the hearing, they were surrounded by grieving parents holding photos of their deceased children.

Meta CEO Mark Zuckerberg responded to the onslaught of grief by apologizing after pressure from a senator to admit Meta's wrongdoing. Zuckerberg said, "I'm sorry for everything you have all been through. No one should have to go through the things that your families have suffered, and this is why we invested so much."[2]

As parents, you need to educate your children. Social media influencers don't endorse delayed gratification because they make money through advertisement, and brand deals. Instilling in your child both the knowledge of what delayed gratification is, and why it's important, helps them have a social media shield. They are less likely to fall prey to online influencers vying for their attention and money.

WHAT'S A GOOD WAY TO EXPLAIN DELAYED GRATIFICATION TO A YOUNG KID?

When my daughter was young, I told her a story about two squirrels. The story goes like this: To prepare for winter in colder months, squirrels typically store away food, especially acorns, during the fall months. As the colorful leaves on the trees started falling, one squirrel began collecting acorns from oak tree to oak tree to stockpile acorns for the long, harsh winter months. The other squirrel took a more carefree approach. He didn't worry about saving for the future as he thought he had plenty of time. Instead, he spent time soaking up the sun, lounging and eating lots of acorns.

When the snow began to fall, this squirrel had no stockpile of acorns like his neighboring squirrel. He grew weary and thin, and barely survived the winter. When spring finally arrived and the snow melted, he vowed to always be careful about planning for the future. He realized that excess savings (the good kind of excess) would have made his life much easier. He learned the lesson of delayed gratification the hard way. You don't want your kid to be the squirrel that didn't save.

Teaching our kids about delayed gratification is one of the most valuable lessons we can offer them. By educating them about the different ways a dollar can be used—spending, investing, saving and giving away—we are not just teaching them about money but also about making thoughtful, balanced decisions in life.

Think of it like providing a balanced diet. Just as you wouldn't feed your child only steak or only cake, you wouldn't allow them to manage money by focusing solely on spending. A balanced meal includes all the essential food groups in the right proportions, which nourishes the body and supports growth. Similarly, a balanced approach to money teaches kids to nourish their financial health, supporting their growth into responsible, successful adults.

Guiding our children through this process is crucial. When we actively lead them in these exercises—whether it's setting aside money for different purposes or discussing the importance of each—we are helping them develop a discipline that will benefit them for the rest of their lives.

We can reinforce this concept in everyday situations. For example, at the dinner table, we can discuss how we allocate money in our household—how much goes to bills, how much is saved, and how much is invested.

If we allow our children to spend all the money they receive, we are setting them up for a potential future of financial instability. Spending without saving or investing can lead to financial strain, just as a diet of only cake can lead to poor health. By teaching our kids to regulate their spending and make thoughtful decisions with their money, we are equipping them with the skills they need to thrive. The time we invest in teaching our children about delayed gratification and financial discipline is one of the greatest gifts we can give them.

HOW EASY IS IT TO TEACH KIDS THE REWARDS OF DELAYED GRATIFICATION IN THIS INSTANT GRATIFICATION WORLD?

Understand there may be resistance to delayed gratification. As you know, kids naturally resist a lot of things. As a parent, you are already familiar with showing them the rewards and consequences of their actions. For example, if they clean their room, they can go to the playground or out on Friday night with their friends. If they don't, they have to stay home.

When my daughter was on the high school tennis team, she resisted going to practice. I told her, "Okay, if you don't practice, your skill will suffer and your ranking will go down." She realized the importance of practice even though she didn't always want to go.After her team won a big tournament, I asked her if it was worth it. She responded, "Yes, 100 percent." It was a valuable lesson in how if you put in the effort, you'll reap the reward, just like saving and investing money.

By encouraging my daughter to go to practice, I was teaching her the connection between wanting something and getting it, the significance of earning something, not just receiving something with little or no effort.

Most kids can't resist the allure of candy as it's typically a special treat for them. If a kid grows up in a family where candy is always available, it is no longer a special treat and the value diminishes. They feel entitled to the treat without working for it. You can apply the same concept to money. When ultra-wealthy families throw money at their kids, the children grow up not seeing the value of money, distorting their future perspective. Because children raised in this environment don't have to work for money, chances are they won't respect money.

By contrast, families living paycheck to paycheck often feel trapped in a cycle where saving or investing seems impossible. They might say things like, "I'm barely getting by," or "I don't have any extra to save or invest." This scarcity mindset is common among those who struggle to make ends meet, and it's understandable. However, the deeper issue at play is the lesson these struggling parents are teaching their kids.

People who buy lottery tickets tend to be people who live paycheck to paycheck. It's not uncommon to see people who are struggling financially spending their last few dollars hoping to win big. It stems from a mix of desperation and hope—the belief that a windfall could solve all their financial problems.

Improving your financial situation might require significant sacrifices, such as taking on a second job, downsizing your living space or making other tough decisions to reduce expenses. By involving your children in these decisions—explaining why the family is choosing to live more frugally—you're teaching them the importance of prioritizing long-term stability over short-term gratification. When your kids see progress, they begin to understand that small sacrifices today can lead to significant rewards tomorrow. You are setting them up for a lifetime of financial stability and success.

Remember, it's not just what you say—it's also what you do that truly shapes your children's beliefs and behaviors. Kids are perceptive, and they pay far more attention to your actions than to your words. If you struggle with money or have a scarcity mindset, your kids will notice. They'll see how you manage finances, how you talk about money and how you react to financial stress. Over time, they may internalize these behaviors and adopt a similar outlook on money.

For example, if you are constantly stressed about finances, cutting corners, and avoiding discussions about money, your kids might grow up believing that financial struggle is a normal, inevitable part of life. They may develop a fear-based relationship with money. This mindset can limit their potential and keep them trapped in the same financial struggles you've experienced.

However, if you approach finances with a mindset of abundance, you're planting seeds of possibility in your children's minds. You're showing them that money is not something to be feared, but a tool that can be managed, grown and used to create opportunities.

When you bring your children along on your financial journey, you're doing more than just teaching them about money—you're showing them how to approach life's challenges with resilience. You're opening up a universe of possibilities.

To give your young child a taste of what excess might look like in their lives, supply them with two clear jars. Explain, "Here's the deal. For every dollar you earn from your allowance or gifts, you are going to put half in each jar. The first jar contains money you can spend right away on things you want. The second jar is saving money to invest in the future—that's your excess money which is super important. Excess money gives you financial freedom because you are saving for your future."

When you do this, you are building your child's money

muscles early on so that they instinctively don't spend all their money right away, and there's always enough money for the future.

CAN THE IDEA OF EXCESS MONEY ENCOURAGE YOUR KID TO BECOME AN ENTREPRENEUR?

Excess money can encourage your child to become curious about starting an entrepreneurial venture, such as a babysitting service or lemonade stand. It's easy for kids to understand the idea of earning money as a business. They sell something (like lemonade) or perform a service (like walking a dog) and earn money.

How many customers they serve, or the amount of money they earn, isn't necessarily going to determine how successful their business will be. Rather, what determines the success of their business is what they do with the money, *not how much money they make.*

This concept applies both to owning a business, and to what your child does when they earn money or are given money as a gift. Do they save some of it or spend it all? These kinds of money habits get formed early on and heavily influence how they view and handle money throughout their lives.

Excess money has incredible value. If your kids can find ways that create value and money—operating like they are a business—it will help them understand excess money much more easily. Discuss the importance of saving and investing profit wisely. Just as your kids save their allowance to buy something they really want, businesses save their profits to reinvest in the business or save for unexpected expenses.

Explain that owning a business involves taking risks. Sometimes, the lemonade stand might need to close because it's raining unexpectedly. On other days, there may be a surplus of money because it's a perfectly sunny day, and there is more foot traffic because of the farmer's market down the street.

IN OUR BUY NOW/PAY LATER SOCIETY, HOW DO YOU GET YOUR KID EXCITED ABOUT THE FUTURE?

As a parent, you want to promote the conversation by saying your kids have choices on what they can do with their excess cash. Explain how excess cash allows them to:

- Reinvest their money
- Make more money
- Create value
- Practice discipline and delayed gratification
- See a benefit in the future that outweighs the sacrifices they are making now

The perks of having excess money include:

- Long-term financial security
- Investment opportunities
- Freedom and flexibility
- Peace of mind
- The ability to give back to the community

Real estate mogul Robert Kiyosaki, author of *Rich Dad, Poor Dad,* shares how starting investing sooner has a more powerful compounding effect over time. Compounding returns happen when the money you earn from your investments (like interest or profits) is added back to your original amount. This means you start earning money on the money you've already made, not just on what you initially invested.

In a garden, each element interacts to create a healthier whole. Trees provide shade to protect delicate flowers, shrubs offer shelter and flowers bring beauty and diversity. In your financial portfolio, each asset class—stocks, bonds, and real estate—can similarly work together to foster compounding growth. Reinvesting dividends from stocks, interest from bonds and income from real estate creates a cycle of growth that benefits all areas of your financial life.

Here's how it works:

- Imagine you invest $100.
- If you earn 10 percent in a year, you get $10 in interest.
- You reinvest by not taking the $10 and instead keep it in your account.
- The following year you earn 10 percent on $110, which is $11 so now you have $121 in your account.

It works well because the longer you keep your money invested, the more it grows because you're earning on your earnings. Once you set it up, you can let it grow without doing much. By leaving it alone, your earnings stay invested and grow. Compounding returns help your money grow faster by allowing you to earn money on your earnings over time!

Lou Grubb knows something about making sacrifices for compounding returns. He was something of a legend in the Phoenix area, known for his folksy commercials touting his local car dealerships. Meeting Lou Grubb remains one of the highlights of my career. He embodied the ultra-rich lifestyle, from how he ran his dealerships to how he managed his life.

Grubb moved to Phoenix in 1945. A few years later, he landed a job as a junior salesman at a Ford dealership. In 1972, he was presented with the opportunity to buy it. Given his frugal spending strategy, he was the only one of his peers with the savings to do so. He was on the right side of leveraging.

Grubb's initial purchase turned into a car dealership conglomerate that he would later sell to AutoNation in 1997 for a fortune. He was so popular that in 1977, Arizona Republicans courted him to run for governor, which he declined, preferring to focus on his business.

The most important detail here is that Grubb was not the

only one who received the initial opportunity to purchase the dealership. His fellow managers also received the offer.

Lou could have had at least one business partner in that deal, potentially even two or three. But because Lou had lived frugally for so long, he was the only employee who had built up enough savings to be able to purchase when the time came. The other managers lived paycheck to paycheck, always buying the latest, greatest new toys.

What was the result? They ended up working for Grubb as wage earners and could never experience the type of financial freedom that he did.

Instead of spending on a more lavish lifestyle like his fellow managers, Grubb saved a lot of money and lived in a modest home. This allowed him to make a deal that wasn't overly leveraged and ultimately, to grow his wealth by becoming an owner.

Through all of this, Grubb carried no personal or business debt and gave back to his community. He died in 2012 at the age of 89. Through the years, he taught his family about money management and kept his investments simple, paving the way for his kids to understand and play the money game as wisely as he had.

You can teach your child the same principles by getting them to understand the power of earning interest.

HOW CAN PLAYING VIDEO GAMES TRANSLATE TO A LESSON ON INVESTING?

A friend of mine has a kid who is an avid gamer, and especially loves *Call of Duty*. I told him this was a perfect opportunity to teach his kid about the power of investing.

When a new version of *Call of Duty* came out, this kid was first to purchase it (he would do chores for four weeks just so he could buy the latest edition). As a consumer, he bought the game for $70, will most likely play it for six months, and then most likely there will be a new version that he'll want. Though he was a consumer in this context, there was an opportunity here for my friend to help his son become an investor, too.

My friend offered to help his son purchase shares of Activision stock (the company that creates *Call of Duty*). By doing so, he explained that they would both become owners who benefit from all the people who buy *Call of Duty*. The more people that buy *Call of Duty*, the more the stock increases in value. My friend's kid was intrigued, and he and his dad had a great conversation about what investing can look like when you are passionate about something.

My friend started the conversation by saying, "Wouldn't it be cool if you put $100 of your money into Activision and watched it grow to $150?" That's when he explained how stocks work and how investment values go up and down over time, but often go up over a more extended period. The waiting required is why instant gratification doesn't bode well for acquiring excess cash which is the next chapter's focus.

Investing is a game of consistency. It requires the same type of discipline an athlete needs to reach their full potential and succeed in their respective sport. It's all about delayed gratification and learning to say no when all you want to do is say yes. Of course, there are tradeoffs. But, to acquire financial freedom, your child will be saying no to their friends much more than yes.

As their parents, you'll continue to highlight the future benefits of what your kids can earn through saving and investing excess cash. This leads to another concept your kid should appreciate: earning money by not doing anything and using that money for assets, not buying possessions. We'll explore that in the next chapter.

KEY TAKEAWAYS

- Excess cash provides your kids with future opportunities and freedom.
- Kids need to learn discipline in order to make excess cash work for them.
- Business success is more about what you do with your excess money, not how much money you make.
- Learn and earn assets to find freedom.

CHAPTER 12
MONEY IN THE MAIL: BUILDING PASSIVE INCOME

"If you don't find a way to make money while you sleep, you will work until you die."
—Warren Buffett

LESSON: PASSIVE INCOME MAKES YOU MONEY WHILE YOU SLEEP.

Want to pique your kid's interest when it comes to living a lifestyle of financial freedom? Ask them to imagine going to the mailbox and earning a paycheck without having to work for it. That's passive income—the polar opposite of earned income.

It's like having two distinct buckets. The earned income bucket is the money you get from doing chores or jobs. The other bucket is the money that comes to you automatically without having to work for it. The difference lies in where the money is coming from and the effort required to make that money.

BUCKET 1: EARNED INCOME

With earned income, you are trading your time, skills and effort directly for money.

I explain it this way to kids, "When you earn an allowance by doing chores around the house, like doing the dishes or taking out the trash, that's earned income. You did the work, so you earned that money. Grown-ups have jobs like teacher, construction worker, lawyer or retail store clerk. The money they get paid from doing their job is their earned income. They have to go to work to get paid. It's money worked for and earned through labor."

BUCKET 2: PASSIVE INCOME OR ASSET INCOME

The goal of passive income is to create a source of recurring revenue that grows over time and provides a steady stream of income without the need for active work. Teaching children about passive income early on empowers them with valuable financial knowledge and instills crucial entrepreneurial skills.

I explain it to kids this way, "The neat thing about passive income is that it's money that keeps coming to you automatically, even when you're not working at that moment. It's like a money tree that grows and gives you more money over time without having to do much work." Instead of telling your kids that money doesn't grow on trees, you can let them know that money can grow on trees if you plant the seeds of investment well and nurture those seeds.

The ultimate goal is to build passive income. As your investment assets and passive cash flow grows, you have more and more financial freedom. A healthy passive income can even fully or partially fund your lifestyle.. As a parent, you may have never experienced this kind of freedom, but it's not too late to encourage your kids to do so.

Instead of having your kids expend energy following others on social media, encourage them to concentrate on growing their net worth through passive income. Engage their imagination on the what ifs. Have conversations like: "What if you never had to worry about money? What would your ideal life look like based on what you value?" Financial planners often ask their clients these kinds of questions to determine what matters most to them and then create a financial plan around it. If your kids can grasp the concept of today's pleasures versus tomorrow's freedom, it can give them a healthy financial trajectory.

As your kids begin to share with you about what they value most and how this might be part of their ideal lifestyle, the next question is how they can make this a reality.

WHAT'S THE BEST WAY TO SHOW HOW TO EARN PASSIVE INCOME?

In one word—assets. Assets generate passive income through either appreciation, income or both. Assets are a revenue stream that can help your child improve their life, achieve their goals and build their future without having to only rely on trading time for money.

Growing assets takes time. You aren't going to get six pack abs in a week. It takes consistent effort to achieve this goal. The same philosophy applies to assets. Acquiring assets requires discipline, and it requires resisting the urge to buy the latest and greatest thing just because it seems like everybody else is.

You'll want your kids to have at least a basic understanding of what assets are, what assets can do for them and why not all assets are created equally. There are two different types of assets —depreciating and appreciating. They are polar opposites as one goes up and the other goes down in value:

Appreciating assets increase in value over time.

Real estate is one of the most popular appreciating assets because it tends to increase in value over time. Different types of real estate—including residential, commercial, industrial and land—can appreciate in value. Real estate also offers the potential for rental income. You could be a landlord or owner of a short-term rental property.

To explain the concept of appreciating assets to your child, you could say, "Imagine you bought a property and have people renting from you and paying your bills and mortgage. Because of that, you get the benefit of real estate appreciation and money in the mail each month. Can you imagine what it would feel like to have an appreciating asset like real estate?" While real estate markets can experience short-term fluctuations, properties in well-chosen locations often show steady long-term growth. (We'll get more into real estate in Chapter 14.)

Depreciating assets lose value over time.

For example, a new bike or video game console becomes worth less the older it gets because newer models come out. Items that get worn out or outdated are depreciating assets. Social media influencers love to push depreciating assets like jewelry, clothes and shoes because they get a kickback from the manufacturers for doing so.

There's no denying the adrenaline rush from purchasing something new, whether it's a new outfit, car or house. The problem is that it doesn't last. In my financial courses, I always say that possessions are like bananas. They have a short shelf life, then they get brown and rotten. Whatever you buy gets stale and lacks the long-term luster you are looking for.

A conversation with your kid might go something like this:"When you buy things that go down in value, you are depleting your money instead of putting your money into an asset that grows. For example, cars are one of the biggest depreciating assets. Brand new cars lose value very quickly, especially in those first few years of ownership as they depreciate between 20-30 percent from the moment you drive off the lot. Even the value of things like a new skateboard that you buy for $100 goes down in value each time you use it. Your skateboard might be worth only $10 when you sell it."

IS THERE A FORMULA TO CALCULATE HOW MUCH PASSIVE INCOME YOU'D NEED TO SUSTAIN A LIFESTYLE?

There's something called the 4% rule which is a popular withdrawal strategy used in retirement income planning. It provides a guideline for how much retirees can theoretically withdraw from their portfolios each year without depleting their nest egg over a 30-year retirement. Even though we aren't referring to retirement per se, the 4% rule can be helpful here.

Assets are like trees. They start out as seedlings and then grow, flourish and produce. In general, assets can generate a sustainable return of about 4%. For example, if you invest $1 million, you can generate about $40,000 a year in perpetual income. So, that's $40,000 you earn each year without doing anything. If you have $2 million, you can earn $80,000. You get the idea.

To figure out how much passive income you'd need to sustain your current lifestyle without trading your time for money, estimate how much you spend each year and divide it by .04%. So, if you spent $100,000 each year, you'd need to invest $2.5 million in assets to generate that $100,000 annually without working. And if you spent $500,000 each year, you'd need to invest $12.5 million in assets to generate that amount. The bottom line is the more extravagant your lifestyle, the more money you need to sustain it.

Ideally, you want investments to generate a return either in appreciation or in income, both of which are money in the mail. When you create excess dollars, turn around and reinvest them. If you do that consistently, the paycheck from your investments (your passive income) will become greater than your earned income. When that happens, you hit a crossover or inflection point called freedom. Financial freedom is getting to wake up every day and do things by choice, not by need.

HOW DO YOU KEEP THE ENTHUSIASM GOING, SINCE PASSIVE INCOME DOESN'T MATERIALIZE IMMEDIATELY?

Keep asking your kids what passions of theirs could benefit from passive income. Ask them what their best life looks like, one where they have the time and freedom to do what they really want.

Depending on your child's age, you can have conversations like, "So, would you like to live a life of freedom and choice, or would you like to live a life where you have to do things based on a lifestyle that you have to support?" Explain that every financial decision they make plays into this, whether it's the type of apartment they live in, the kind of car they drive or the clothes they wear.

Financial freedom is an option all our kids deserve, but so few are exposed to the how of financial freedom at an early age. I can't tell you how many of my students lament that they didn't learn about passive income and how to handle money until they were well into their adulthood.

As your kid's parent, keep encouraging them and keep having these regular money conversations as they build their assets.

KEY TAKEAWAYS

- Depreciating assets are like bananas. They have a short shelf life, and then they get brown and rotten. Aim for appreciating assets instead.
- Money in the mail generates income while you sleep.
- Use the 4% rule to calculate how much money you need in assets to sustain your desired lifestyle.
- Download the Free Cash Flow Worksheet at www.401kid.education.

CHAPTER 13

HOW TO PLANT A FOREVER GARDEN THAT BLOOMS EQUITY VERSUS DEBT

"The biggest risk of all is not taking one."
—Mellody Hobson

LESSON: STOCKS, BONDS AND REAL ESTATE ARE THE MOST COMMON assets when it comes to investing.

In the landscape of life, we are all gardeners. Our decisions, choices and investments are the seeds we plant. Over time, with care, those seeds blossom into the fruits of our labor. When it comes to building wealth, the garden metaphor becomes especially powerful, as managing investments wisely resembles tending to a well-designed garden.

The three essential elements of any financial garden are stocks, bonds and real estate. They grow, balance and complement each other over time.

Patience and discipline are key in both gardening and investing. If you weather the occasional drought and keep tending to your financial garden, you'll be rewarded with a bountiful harvest down the road. It may start small, but with dedication, your investments can flourish and yield a fruitful future.

WHAT ARE SOME ASSETS TO SHARE WITH YOUR KIDS TO GET THEM STARTED ON THEIR FINANCIAL JOURNEY?

When it comes to investing, there are three main options: stocks, bonds and real estate. If you want to build a strong and balanced investment portfolio, you'll need to understand stock, bonds and real estate.

STOCKS: FAST-GROWING, COLORFUL FLOWERS

Stocks are often the first investment people think of when they consider growing their wealth, and for good reason. Like fast-growing, eye-catching flowers, stocks can bloom quickly, producing beautiful results in a short amount of time. But, just like flowers that may be affected by changing weather, stocks are often subject to unpredictable market conditions.

Stocks represent ownership in a company. When you buy a stock, you essentially own a small part of that business, sharing in its profits and growth. The stock market often rewards investors handsomely for their risk, and stocks have historically offered the highest returns of any mainstream investment option. They grow quickly, much like vibrant flowers reaching toward the sun. However, as with flowers that are vulnerable to the elements, stock prices can fluctuate wildly based on economic cycles, corporate performance and investor sentiment.

> **Potential for High Growth:** Stocks are dynamic and growth-oriented, offering the chance for substantial wealth accumulation over time. The value of your stock can increase significantly if the company performs well, much like a flower blooming in the right conditions.

> **Short-Term Volatility:** While stocks provide the highest

returns in the long term, they are the most volatile in the short term. One day, the market may be booming, and your garden is in full bloom. The next day, unexpected events like an economic downturn may feel like a cold frost, causing your stock values to wither, even if only temporarily.

Like flowers, stocks require your attention and patience. While you can't control the overall market climate, you can select healthy "flowers" by choosing well-managed companies with solid growth potential. Diversifying the types of stocks you hold is like planting various flowers that thrive in different conditions, ensuring your garden remains colorful and growing even when certain sectors of the market struggle.

It's crucial to not overwater—meaning, avoid obsessively checking your stocks every day or reacting impulsively to market fluctuations. Just as over-nurturing can harm plants, overreacting to short-term volatility can hinder your ability to enjoy the long-term growth stocks provide.

WHAT IS THE DIFFERENCE BETWEEN STOCKS AND BONDS?

Stocks can boost your earnings potential, while bonds help keep things steady and secure—perfect for different phases in your financial life.

Let's return to our garden metaphor. When you buy stocks, you're planting the seeds of ownership in different companies, just like sowing seeds in your garden. When you invest in real estate, it's like growing a fruit tree on your own plot of land.

Think of the stocks you purchase as seedlings and saplings in your garden. Small-cap stocks are like the delicate, fast-growing annual plants—they have lots of potential for big growth, but they can also be more fragile and prone to risks. Meanwhile, large-cap stocks are like sturdy, slow-growing trees and shrubs in your garden. They may not grow as quickly, but they tend to be more stable over time.

As those stock "seedlings" take root and the companies start performing well, the value of your investments can blossom. When the overall stock market is thriving, it's like optimal growing conditions for all the plants in your investment garden. But when there are economic downturns or company-specific challenges, it can lead to a bit of a rough patch. Think of it like a drought or pest infestation in your real-life garden.

The key is to tend to your investment garden with care, just as you would your actual garden. Diversifying your portfolio, like planting a variety of fruits, vegetables and flowers, helps spread out the risks. Regularly checking in and pruning or "rebalancing" your investments, like weeding and monitoring your garden, keeps your whole plot healthy and productive.

With patience and persistence, the seeds you plant in the form of stocks and real estate can grow into a bountiful harvest over time. It may take some work, but carefully cultivating your financial garden can yield big rewards.

WHAT ARE THE RISKS AND REWARDS WHEN IT COMES TO STOCKS?

Investing in stocks is a bit like cultivating a vegetable garden—it has the potential to yield a bountiful harvest, but you have to carefully navigate the inherent risks and unpredictable factors along the way.

The chance to score big with stocks is akin to growing a bumper crop of your favorite produce. When the conditions are right and the plants thrive, you can reap an incredible bounty. Just like a healthy, well-tended plant producing an abundance of juicy tomatoes or crisp cucumbers, a successful company's stock price can skyrocket, allowing savvy investors to profit well over time.

The dividends paid out by certain stocks are similar to the

steady stream of fresh produce you can harvest from your garden throughout the growing season. It's a nice, reliable income boost, much like being able to regularly pick and enjoy the fruits of your labor in the garden.

However, the risks associated with stocks are like the unpredictable challenges that can arise in any garden. Market conditions can cause dramatic swings in stock prices, just as a sudden drought or heatwave can devastate your vegetable plants. Company performance is like the health of your garden. If you don't cultivate your garden well or it becomes infested with pests and disease, your yields (and stock value) can plummet.

External events, whether natural disasters or a global pandemic, can wreak havoc on both stock prices and garden productivity, leaving investors and gardeners vulnerable to significant losses.

The key to successfully navigating the risks and rewards of stocks is patience and a long-term perspective. Jumping in and out based on short-term fluctuations is like constantly uprooting your garden—it's a recipe for disappointment. But those who are willing to ride out the inevitable ups and downs, tending diligently to their investments, are more likely to see their portfolios flourish over time, just as a well-cared-for garden yields bounty season after season.

WHAT ARE SOME OF THE DIFFERENT TYPES OF STOCKS TO ADD TO THE GARDEN OF INVESTMENT OPTIONS?

Just like plants in a garden, stocks are diverse, with each type of investment offering unique risks and rewards. The following are the main categories of stocks:

Blue-Chip Stocks: Imagine that blue-chip stocks are sturdy, well-established trees. These trees have deep roots and a history of enduring seasons, much like companies such as Apple, Microsoft and Coca-Cola. They're reliable, stable and often bear fruit in the form of regular dividends. While they may not grow as rapidly as some plants in the garden, their steady presence provides a sense of security in your investment landscape.

Growth Stocks: Think of growth stocks as sunflowers that flourish with rapid growth as they stretch towards the sun. Like sunflowers, growth stocks are expected to grow faster than average. Instead of producing seeds (or dividends) to share with gardeners, they reinvest their energy and resources into growing taller and producing more sunflowers. While the growth can be exciting, it comes with risks. If conditions aren't right, those vibrant sunflowers could wilt quickly, leading to a significant drop in their visual appeal—much like a growth stock declining if it fails to meet expectations.

Value Stocks: Value stocks are like hidden perennials in the garden. They might not draw attention at first but possess the potential for breathtaking blooms. These plants, often overlooked, represent companies that are undervalued and are waiting for the right conditions to blossom. Investors who cultivate value stocks eagerly seek out hidden gems, hoping that in time, the market will recognize their worth and they will flourish.

Small and Mid-Sized Stocks: Keeping with our garden theme, small and mid-sized stocks resemble young saplings and spry shrubs. Being in their developmental stages, these plants can be a bit more vulnerable to harsh weather conditions and pests (economic fluctuations). Yet, they also hold the potential for exciting growth spurts as smaller companies often have more room to expand and flourish. Investing in these saplings might be

riskier, but the potential for a bountiful harvest
is tempting.

Dividend Stocks: Think of dividend stocks as berry
bushes that not only grow beautifully but also bear valuable fruit. These plants provide a continual yield,
rewarding gardeners regularly for their care. Just as you
can harvest berries without uprooting the bush, dividend
stocks allow shareholders to benefit from regular payouts
without having to sell their shares. For those seeking a
steady stream of income while nurturing their garden,
these stocks offer not only sweet returns but also the
chance to reinvest and watch their garden of wealth
expand over time. However, while these berry bushes are
rewarding, they might not produce the biggest crops if
their energy goes more into fruit production than growth.

Just like every type of plant contributes to the beauty and
diversity of a garden, various types of stocks fill the investment
landscape with opportunities, each with its own blend of risk
and reward.

WHAT ARE WAYS TO HANDLE INVESTMENT RISKS TO CULTIVATE A FINANCIAL GARDEN?

Just like tending to a garden requires careful planning and
nurturing, the same applies to managing stock market risks to
receive a bountiful harvest. The following are different investment strategies.

DIVERSIFICATION: PLANT A VARIETY OF SEEDS

Imagine you're planting a garden with a mix of flowers and
vegetables. If one type of plant fails due to poor weather or
pests, the others can still thrive, providing you with a steady

crop. The same strategy applies to the stock market where diversification is key.

By spreading your investments across different types of stocks, industries and asset classes, you reduce the threat posed by any single underperforming investment. This variety can help maintain the overall health of your financial garden.

A healthy garden thrives on diversity. A garden filled with only fast-growing flowers may look beautiful in the spring, but when the seasons change, it may be left barren. The same is true for a financial portfolio that consists only of one type of investment, such as stocks. Without the balance provided by bonds and real estate, it could become vulnerable to market downturns.

Diversification in your financial garden is the equivalent of planting various species of plants, each suited to different conditions. Stocks (flowers) may offer quick and vibrant growth but are prone to the whims of the market. Bonds (shrubs) provide stability and protection, while real estate (trees) offers long-term growth and income.

By diversifying, you're not placing all your bets on one plant or one type of investment. When one investment falters, another may thrive. For instance, if the stock market enters a downturn, your bonds and real estate may remain steady, balancing the overall portfolio.

THINKING LONG-TERM: NURTURE GROWTH OVER TIME

Just as some plants take longer to bloom and bear fruit, investing in stocks is about patience. By adopting a long-term investment strategy, you give your investments the time needed to weather market fluctuations. Just like gardeners know that tough seasons will eventually give way to fruitful yields, investors who stay the course often see their patience rewarded with attractive returns over time.

REGULAR INVESTING: CONSISTENT WATERING

Think about how a garden flourishes with regular watering. In the investing world, this is called regular investing. When you consistently invest, you're essentially watering your financial garden at every stage of growth. This strategy allows you to buy more shares when prices are low and fewer when they're high, potentially lowering your average cost per share—a vital step toward ensuring your garden flourishes in the long run.

REBALANCING: PRUNING FOR OPTIMAL GROWTH

From time to time, gardeners need to prune their plants to encourage growth and prevent overcrowding. Just like pruning your plants, you'll want to prune or rebalance your portfolio as you make adjustments that align with your changing risk tolerance and goals. If one stock has grown too much, like an overly dominant plant in your garden, selling some shares can free up resources to nurture other areas of your portfolio that need attention, keeping everything in balance.

Just like a well-tended garden can yield a variety of blooms and vegetables, stocks can significantly enhance your portfolio's returns. However, the journey can be fraught with ups and downs—much like unpredictable weather affecting your garden. That's why you'll want to understand the different types of stocks and the risks associated with them. By using strategies like diversification and long-term thinking, you can cultivate a robust financial garden.

KEY TAKEAWAYS

- Investing is similar to tending a garden, requiring planning, patience, and nurturing over time.
- Stocks and bonds are two common assets to introduce to kids for starting their financial journey.
- Diversification in investing, like planting a variety of seeds, helps manage risk and maintain overall portfolio health.
- Long-term thinking in investing, akin to nurturing plants over time, often leads to better outcomes.
- Regular investing, like consistent watering, can help lower average costs and promote steady growth.

CHAPTER 14

PLANTING MIGHTY TREES WITH DEEP ROOTS IN REAL ESTATE FOR A FERTILE FINANCIAL LANDSCAPE

"Real estate cannot be lost or stolen, nor can it be carried away. Purchased with common sense, paid for in full, and managed with reasonable care, it is about the safest investment in the world."
—Franklin D. Roosevelt

LESSON: REAL ESTATE INVESTING, LIKE CULTIVATING A GARDEN, requires careful planning, diverse strategies, and ongoing attention to nurture growth and manage risks for long-term success.

In every thriving garden, there are trees. Trees take time to grow, but they stand the test of time, providing shade, shelter and even fruit. Real estate investments operate in much the same way. Though real estate typically grows more slowly compared to stocks, it is a strong and enduring asset class that provides stability and income for generations.

Unlike stocks or bonds, which are more abstract, real estate is a tangible asset. You can see it, walk through it and feel its presence. Just like a towering tree, real estate can provide long-term growth and shelter from the harsh elements of market volatility.

Appreciation Over Time: Real estate grows steadily, much like a tree. It may not shoot up overnight, but over the long term, it can provide significant appreciation in value, especially if the property is located in a growing area. Real estate typically increases in value as demand for land and housing rises, giving your portfolio deep roots.

Income-Generating: Trees also bear fruit, and in the financial garden, rental properties are your income-bearing trees. By renting out properties, you can earn a steady cash flow, much like harvesting fruit year after year. This income is generally less volatile than stock dividends, making it a reliable source of passive income.

A Legacy Investment: Just as trees in a garden can live for generations, real estate can serve as a legacy investment. A well-maintained property can be passed down to children or sold at a later date, providing financial security and a tangible asset for future generations.

Like trees, real estate requires ongoing care. You need to manage properties, whether by tending to tenants, overseeing maintenance or ensuring that the neighborhood continues to grow and thrive. With the right care, your real estate can provide long-term value and serve as a protective force in your portfolio.

PLANTING A REAL ESTATE GARDEN: NURTURING RISK AND REWARD

Just like a gardener seeks fertile ground for a bountiful harvest, real estate investors look for properties with the potential for significant returns. When you plant a seed (invest in a property), you anticipate it will grow over time. As your property appreciates in value, it can lead to a flourishing garden of profits. Just as gardeners enjoy the fruits of their labor, investors can reap the benefits of rental income from tenants—it's like harvesting fresh vegetables each season.

Using leverage in real estate is like putting rich compost in your garden. By borrowing money, you can cultivate a larger plot than you could with your own resources alone. Now you can expand your garden's potential yield. Just as a well-fertilized garden can produce more vibrant blooms, investing with leverage can amplify your returns, especially if the value of your property appreciates.

Be aware that cultivating your real estate garden isn't without challenges. Just as weeds can choke your plants, various risks can threaten your investment. The market can be unpredictable, much like the weather that can stomp on a gardener's optimism. If property values plummet due to economic downturns or shifts in local demand, you might find yourself facing losses similar to a crop failure when conditions turn against you.

Liquidity risk in real estate is like waiting for your harvest to ripen; selling a property isn't a quick process. If you need cash rapidly, it may take a while to find a buyer, leaving you with fewer options—just as a gardener might struggle to sell their produce before it spoils. If you rush to sell, the return might be less than desired.

Property-specific risks are like pests or diseases that can infest a garden. Unexpected maintenance costs, legal disputes, or changes in zoning laws can drain resources, just like blight can ruin a perfect row of tomatoes. If you're renting out properties, your challenge will be finding reliable tenants. Without them, your cash flow—and overall profits—can wither.

Using leverage can be a double-edged sword, similar to installing a trellis to support climbing plants. While it can help maximize your garden space and lead to greater yields, it also introduces risk. Should property values diminish, you might find yourself in an "underwater" situation. Think of it like a trellis collapsing under the weight of too many vines. If rental income decreases or unexpected expenses arise, managing your "garden" could become a struggle, risking foreclosure just as a gardener faces losing their entire plot to neglect.

With careful planning, attention, and an understanding of the risks and rewards, you can cultivate a real estate investment that yields fruitful returns. But, stay vigilant against the weeds, pests, and unexpected weather and don't forget to pack your patience.

Just as you choose the right seeds, soil and conditions to maximize your harvest in a garden, selecting the right type of real estate investment will help you cultivate a thriving financial future. You'll want to consider the following:

HOUSING MARKET: THE FLOWER BED

In your garden, a flower bed filled with colorful blooms represents the housing market. Consider single-family homes to be like easy-to-grow daisies and tulips, perfect for novice gardeners. They require minimal care and can flourish beautifully, offering a steady return like a blooming flower each season. However, you must be wary of unexpected maintenance issues or market shifts just as a gardener must be wary of pests or poor weather.

Consider multi-family properties to resemble a patch of mixed perennials. While they provide a more abundant harvest of flowers (rental income), they require more effort to tend to. If one flower wilts and fades however, you still have others thriving which give you a consistent bloom throughout the season. The same applies to having multiple rental units. Owning multiple units shields you from losing income if one tenant moves out.

COMMERCIAL REAL ESTATE: THE GREENHOUSE

Commercial real estate acts like a greenhouse, where various plants may flourish under controlled conditions. Think of office and retail spaces as representing exotic plants that need specific climates (long leases and steady economic conditions) to thrive. When the economy is booming, these spaces bloom beautifully, but they can struggle during harsh conditions like economic downturns.

Think of industrial properties as hardy crops that are less affected by seasonal changes—they are dependable and bring a steady yield under long-term leases. However, industry shifts can still affect them much like certain crops might struggle if soil conditions suddenly change.

REAL ESTATE INVESTMENT TRUSTS (REITS): THE SEED BANK

Think of REITs as a seed bank that allows you to invest in a variety of plant species (real estate) without having to dig in the soil yourself. You can explore different types of seeds. Equity REITs are like flowering plants that bear fruit (providing dividends and growth). Mortgage REITs (mREITs) resemble sturdy tree seeds that offer robust interest returns but need careful oversight due to shifting weather conditions (interest rates). Finally, there are hybrid REITs which are like a well-mixed seed pack bringing together the best features of both flowers and sturdy trees.

BUILDING STUFF: PREPARING THE PLOT

Real estate development is like preparing a new plot in your garden. It requires a solid plan and investment (cash) to lay the ground before planting anything. The potential rewards are rich, like a bountiful harvest, but the risks are substantial as well. You need to take into consideration unpredictable weather (market demand) and know which permits (approvals) to apply for.

VACATION RENTALS: THE SEASONAL CROP

Vacation rentals are like planting seasonal crops, which can flourish in the summer months when tourists return, bringing in plenty of sunlight (income). Just as gardeners must manage the ups and downs of seasonal yields, owners of vacation rentals need to navigate varying demand. They need to stay updated on local regulations, ensuring their garden (property) stays appealing and accessible to travelers.

Just like a gardener assesses soil, weather and plant varieties to create a thriving garden, an investor must look at the different avenues of real estate. By understanding the risks and implementing strategies to mitigate them, you can cultivate a bountiful harvest in investment returns. With the right nurturing, your real estate investments can grow and flourish, providing a sustainable source of wealth over the years.

KEY TAKEAWAYS

- Real estate investing is like planting a grove of trees, where properties appreciate over time and generate income through rent.
- Leverage in real estate is comparable to using compost in a garden, allowing investors to amplify returns but also introducing risks.
- Different types of real estate investments are like various plants in a garden, each with unique characteristics and care requirements.
- Real estate can offer solid returns and tax benefits, but comes with risks such as market fluctuations, liquidity issues and property-specific problems.
- Careful planning, attention to detail, and understanding of risks and rewards are crucial for successful real estate investing, much like tending to a garden.

CHAPTER 15

CULTIVATING RELIABLE PLANTS IN YOUR INVESTMENT GARDEN

"The purpose of investing is to make money in a way that allows you to sleep at night."
—William Bernstein

LESSON: INVESTING DOESN'T NEED TO BE INTIMIDATING; WITH consistency, patience, and a well-laid plan, even novice investors can see their financial garden prosper.

Even the most well-planned garden requires care. You can't simply plant seeds and forget about them. Similarly, your investments require ongoing attention. Over time, some plants may outgrow others, requiring pruning, and some new plants might need to be introduced to fill gaps. This is where rebalancing comes into play in your financial portfolio.

In gardening, if your flowers grow too fast, they may crowd out the shrubs and trees, leaving your garden lopsided. Similarly, if one asset class—such as stocks—grows disproportionately, it can unbalance your portfolio. Regularly rebalancing your portfolio ensures that no single investment dominates and that your financial garden remains diverse and resilient.

Patience is key to growing a thriving garden. Plants take time to grow, and each type of investment matures at its own pace.

While stocks may shoot up quickly, bonds and real estate grow steadily. Over time, the combined effects of compounding will bear fruit. A long-term perspective allows you to see beyond short-term fluctuations and appreciate the gradual growth of your financial garden.

In your investment garden, fixed-income investments—bonds or debt securities—serve as a way to cultivate returns by nurturing your funds for others. When you acquire a bond, you're essentially planting a seed—loaning your money to a government or corporation. In return, you receive regular waterings in the form of interest payments over a set period, plus a promise that your original seed will be returned when it reaches maturity.

These bonds are particularly beneficial if you have short-term goals or want to shield your financial garden from the unpredictable storms of the market. They provide a consistent flow of nutrients and tend to be less volatile than stocks, making them a foundational element in a balanced investment portfolio.

UNDERSTANDING THE RISKS AND REWARDS IN YOUR GARDEN OF INVESTMENTS

Fixed-income investments often grow at a slower rate than stocks, as they are considered less ambitious in their growth potential. Most of your returns come from the regular interest. When the bond matures, it's like harvesting the fruits of your labor—you receive back the original amount you planted. The yield from your fixed-income crops depends on several factors:

Interest Rate: The interest rate, or coupon rate, is like the sunshine that influences your garden. Once the bond is established, this rate remains constant, providing a reliable source of warmth and light throughout the entire season.

Credit Quality: The security of the issuer—like different types of plants—affects how much nourishment you can expect. Well-established entities, like the U.S. government, are like hardy oak trees, offering lower yields because they are seen as safe. However, riskier investments, like less stable companies or governments, promise higher returns to entice you to plant them in your garden.

Maturity: Bonds with longer growth cycles tend to yield better fruits since they are more susceptible to changes in interest rates just like how mature plants adapt to their environment. The longer they grow, the more vulnerable they can be to seasonal shifts like interest rate changes and inflation.

In your investment garden, you'll want to cultivate a mix of stocks and bonds. When tending to fixed income investments, it's essential to be aware of the various weeds and pests that can threaten your flourishing plants. The following are some critical areas to keep an eye on while cultivating your financial garden:

Interest Rate Risk: Think of interest rates as kind of like the impact of weather in your garden. If the sun starts shining more brightly—representing rising rates—older plants (older bonds) may struggle to compete. Say you have a flower that blooms beautifully at a 3% interest rate, but new blooms enter the garden with a 5% return. Suddenly, your 3% flower doesn't look as appealing and may lose some of its value, just like a plant that withers in less favorable conditions. Conversely, if the weather cools down and interest rates drop, your existing plants can thrive and appreciate in value.

Credit Risk: Just as some plants are hardier than others, the creditworthiness of the bond issuer plays a crucial role in your gardening success. If you choose to plant seeds from a struggling company, you run the risk of failing to see a fruitful harvest. This is especially true for the high-yield or "junk" bonds, which offer the allure of higher returns but come with the risk of not blooming at all.

Inflation Risk: Inflation is like pesky weeds that can choke your plants. If these weeds grow faster than your flowers can bloom—meaning the rate of inflation surpasses your bond's interest rates—you may find that your investment yields less value. For example, if you've nurtured a bond that yields 2%, but inflation sprouts to 3%, the value of what you harvest diminishes, leaving you with a less bountiful return.

Liquidity Risk: Just as some plants may take longer to sell at the market than others, liquidity risk refers to the challenge of quickly selling a bond without impacting its price. If you need to make space in your garden or find that you need cash fast, you may struggle to find buyers willing to take your less popular plants. Certain bonds, like corporate ones or those from emerging markets, can be tougher to sell. When the garden experiences a drought —a market downturn—you may have to part with your bonds at a significant loss, much like trying to sell wilted flowers for a reduced price.

Reinvestment Risk: You can compare reinvestment risk to regularly planting seasonal crops. When your flowers (bonds) mature and it's time to plant again, you may have to sow seeds at lower interest rates if the market has changed. Imagine saving a bouquet with a 5% bloom, only to find that as you prepare to replant, the current rate has dropped to 3%. You'll be left with less fertile ground for your next harvest, which can diminish your expected financial yield.

In nurturing your garden of fixed income investments, keep an eye on these potential pitfalls.

CULTIVATING YOUR FIXED INCOME GARDEN: EXPLORING DIFFERENT TYPES AND THEIR GROWTH POTENTIAL

Just as some plants thrive in certain conditions while others need more care, each investment type has its own risk and return profile:

Government Bonds: Government bonds are hardy and reliable, offering the most stable returns with minimal risk. U.S. Treasury bonds are like oaks—they stand tall, backed by the strength of the federal government, making them virtually risk-free in terms of credit. However, much like slow-growing oak trees, their returns aren't usually flashy.

Treasury Bonds: Treasury bonds can last for 20 or 30 years, depending on the type of bond. They pay interest every six months until they mature, and you can sell them before they mature or hold them until they mature. Like a mighty oak tree, expect them to provide steady shade, but don't anticipate an abundance of colorful blooms.

Treasury Notes: These are your medium-sized shrubs, lasting 2 to 10 years. They offer reliability, though again, the growth is steady rather than spectacular.

Treasury Bills (T-Bills): Short-term flowers that bloom for less than a year. They're purchased below face value, with the promise of full value at maturity—think of them as quick-blooming annuals that can bring some immediate satisfaction.

Municipal Bonds: Municipal bonds are like beautiful perennials. They might not always flower as well as the U.S. government bonds, but they provide consistent blooms year after year, with the added bonus of usually being tax-free.

General Obligation Bonds: Consider these the reliable daisies of your garden, backed by the issuing municipality, making them relatively safe.

Revenue Bonds: These bonds depend on specific revenue streams, such as utility payments. Like delicate wildflowers, they can add a pop of color, but they may wilt if the expected revenue doesn't materialize.

Corporate Bonds: Corporate bonds resemble fruit-bearing shrubs, which can yield delicious returns but come with a bit more risk. Companies offer these bonds to nurture their growth, typically providing higher interest rates than government bonds, reflecting the risk associated with their credit quality.

Investment-Grade Bonds: Consider these to be like well-established fruit bushes, producing decent yields without overly risky adventures.

High-Yield Bonds (Junk Bonds): Think of these as the exotic, high-maintenance plants that may yield impressive fruits but require careful tending due to their unpredictable nature—offering higher returns but bearing the risk of not blooming at all.

Mortgage-Backed Securities (MBS): MBS is like a mixed bouquet, providing a variety of returns but bringing some inherent risks. The allure lies in their potential for higher yields, yet with them comes the risk of prepayment (like when homeowners decide to prune early) and credit issues if borrowers can't keep up (like flowers wilting due to drought).

Certificates of Deposit (CDs): CDs resemble the solid rocks in your landscape—stable and secure. They are like the foundational stones of your garden, FDIC-insured, offering low risk but modest returns, much like the rocks that create a durable yet static base for everything else to grow upon.

In the grand scheme of your financial garden, fixed income investments play an essential role, offering stability and a consistent stream of income. While they typically present less risk than stocks, they aren't entirely free of threats. Factors like interest rate changes, credit risks and inflation can affect your garden's health.

As you plan your financial garden, consider your comfort with risk, your investment goals and your time horizon—much like a gardener assessing the sunlight and soil conditions. By understanding the diverse plants in the fixed income realm and their unique risks and returns, you'll be better equipped to cultivate a financial garden that flourishes.

TACKLING INTIMIDATION: EASING INTO YOUR INVESTMENT JOURNEY

One of the most exciting aspects of investing is compounding, which is like cultivating a thriving garden. When you reinvest the fruits of your labor—such as dividends, interest or capital gains—back into your garden, you're not just nurturing your original plants, but also encouraging new growth. It's like a snowball rolling down a hill, picking up more snow and speed as it becomes bigger.

Many people find investing intimidating, but cultivating your financial garden doesn't need to be daunting. With over 25 years of teaching investment principles, I've witnessed countless novice gardeners step into the world of investing feeling confused by complex terms. Yet, by the end of the course, most are pleasantly surprised to discover that growing their investment portfolio is much simpler than they initially thought!

Nurturing your financial garden is about consistency, patience and a well-laid plan. You don't need to be an investment expert to see your financial garden prosper. Focus on the basics: plant seeds regularly in stocks and real estate, save for future growth, and avoid pitfalls like trying to predict seasonal changes (market timing) or chasing after the latest horticultural fads.

To better understand the art of cultivating your investment garden, I recommend exploring books like *The Wealthy Gardener* and *Rich Dad Poor Dad*. These resources are rich in real-world advice about entering the world of wealth-building. The more knowledge you acquire, the more confident you will be in making wise gardening choices for your investments. Just as a well-tended garden continuously provides fresh produce, a solid investment strategy can bring you bountiful returns year after year.

While investing might seem intimidating initially, over time, it becomes easier to manage. The essential steps are to get started early, stay focused and continue learning. By doing so, you'll not only cultivate a healthy financial garden for the future, but you'll also feel more relaxed and confident in knowing you're nurturing your financial landscape. Approach investing as a journey—armed with the right mindset and a set of smart strategies, you can cultivate and harvest genuine wealth over time.

SOWING SEEDS: STARTING SMALL

Every gardener knows that any grand garden begins with a single seed. If you're stepping into the world of investments, starting with small seeds is completely natural. As you plant your financial seeds and watch them take root, they can remind you that patience and care are key components of growth.

A 25-year-old might throw around 80-90% of their retirement savings into stocks and just 10-20% into bonds. When they hit 60, they might switch it up to a 50/50 split to play it safe and keep their savings secure.

If you're putting away cash for your kid's education, your investment game plan will change as they get older. In the beginning, you might go all-in on stocks since you've got plenty of time. As college gets closer, it's smart to be a bit more conservative with your investments to make sure your money is ready when you need it.

If you're thinking about buying a home in the next few years, putting your money in a high-yield savings account or a short-term bond fund could be a smart move. They're generally safer and let you access your cash more easily than stocks do.

USING TIME WISELY WHEN INVESTING

Time is a handy tool for investors. It plays a big role in both how much you can earn and how much risk you can handle. When you understand time affects your investments, you can make choices that fit your money goals, comfort with risk and where you're at in life.

When it comes to time and volatility in the markets, you'll want to do the following:

Build Surplus Money: The first step is to establish financial discipline. Without it, you'll never build a surplus.

Once you have a surplus, you have additional "seeds" to plant in your financial garden.

Understand Volatility vs. Risk: Many people confuse the two, often influenced by headlines and short-term market fluctuations. The minute-by-minute movements of the market are mostly just noise—driven by media sensationalism designed to play on fear or greed. They either want you to panic because the returns are bad or make you feel like you're missing out because the returns are good. In reality, markets are quite predictable over the long term. The focus should be on shutting out the noise of the minute-by-minute fluctuations and instead, laying the groundwork for a solid, long-term plan.

Stay Disciplined and Ignore FOMO: Fear of missing out (FOMO) is a significant driver of poor investment decisions. When a particular market category is doing exceptionally well, the media often highlights stories of how many millionaires have resulted from this trend. However, this success is rarely about skill; often it's luck or timing. Success comes from slow and steady growth—consistent nurturing of your financial "garden."

Invest in Real Assets: When you have surplus money, it's essential to invest in real assets—primarily equities or real estate. The key is to stay the course through both up and down markets and not be distracted by short-term noise.

By focusing on these principles, you can teach your kid how to cultivate a sustainable, long-term investment strategy that isn't swayed by short-term trends or emotions.

KEY TAKEAWAYS

- Fixed-income investments (bonds) are like planting seeds that provide regular interest payments and return of principal at maturity, offering stability but typically slower growth than stocks.
- Different types of bonds (government, municipal, corporate) have varying risk-return profiles, just like different plants in a garden.
- Key risks in fixed-income investing include interest rate risk, credit risk, inflation risk, liquidity risk and reinvestment risk.
- Compounding is a powerful force in investing, because reinvesting the fruits of your labor can encourage new growth.
- Continuous learning and focus are essential for cultivating long-term wealth through investing.

CHAPTER 16
KEEPING IT SIMPLE-
CONTINUING TO TEACH
YOUR KIDS ABOUT STOCKS,
REAL ESTATE AND
BUILDING WEALTH

"The most valuable things in life are usually the simplest."
—Norman Vincent Peale

LESSON: BY TEACHING KIDS SIMPLE YET EFFECTIVE PRINCIPLES, parents can set them on a path to financial success while emphasizing that complexity is not necessary for achieving good investment outcomes.

One of the most valuable lessons you can teach your children is that *simplicity is key* when it comes to investing. The financial world may seem overwhelming, but successful investing doesn't require complex strategies or insider knowledge. In fact, the more you simplify the process, the more likely your children are to succeed in the long run. By focusing on a few foundational principles—saving consistently, diversifying wisely and maintaining patience—you can set your kids on a path to building long-term wealth. The key is sticking to a plan and ignoring the distractions that cause many investors to fail.

HOW DOES SIMPLICITY WIN IN INVESTING?

One of the most common mistakes people make when investing is trying to outsmart the market. They think they need to find the perfect stock or predict when the market will rise and fall. But the reality is that timing the market is nearly impossible for even the most seasoned investors. Instead, the most successful investors understand that long-term growth comes from a simple, consistent approach. They don't try to beat the market day to day. Instead, they trust that the market will grow over time and that their diversified investments will pay off.

The following are three core principles of a simple, successful investment strategy that you can pass on to your kids:

1. **Save and Invest Consistently**: The foundation of any investment strategy is saving regularly. The earlier your kids start saving and investing, the more time they'll have to grow their wealth. It's not about how much they start with, it's about building the habit. Teach them that consistently setting aside a portion of their income to invest—no matter how small—will yield big results over time.

2. **Diversify Across Stocks and Real Estate**: Explain to your kids that they don't need to pick individual stocks or follow every trend. Instead, they can invest in *low-cost index funds* that spread their investments across hundreds or thousands of companies. This approach ensures that they're not relying on the success of just a few stocks. By adding real estate to the mix, they gain another asset that grows steadily over time and provides reliable income.

3. **Stay the Course**: The hardest part of investing is not reacting emotionally to the ups and downs of the market. There will always be headlines that make the stock market seem unstable or risky, but reacting to these short-

term events often leads to poor decisions. The key to long-term success is having the patience to stick with their plan, no matter what happens. By investing for the long haul, they'll be able to ride out volatility and come out ahead.

WHAT IS A SIMPLE BREAKDOWN WHEN IT COMES TO THE FOUR QUADRANTS OF STOCK INVESTING?

To make stock investing easier for your kids to understand, you can break it down into four simple categories, or quadrants. Each quadrant represents a different type of stock. By spreading their investments across all four quadrants, they'll reduce their risk while increasing their chances for long-term growth.

1. Large-Cap Stocks: These are shares in large, established companies that are household names—think Apple, Microsoft or Coca-Cola. These companies tend to grow steadily over time, and while they may not experience explosive growth, they are more stable and less volatile than smaller companies. Large-cap stocks are the foundation of a portfolio, offering reliable, steady growth over time.

2. Small-Cap Stocks: Small-cap stocks represent smaller, often newer companies that have the potential for rapid growth. However, they are also more volatile than large-cap stocks, meaning their prices can rise or fall dramatically in a short period. Historically, small-cap stocks have delivered higher returns over the long run, but they require more patience to ride out the bumps. Teach your kids that small-cap stocks are the riskier growth engine of their portfolio, with the potential for higher returns if they're willing to weather short-term volatility.

3. Growth Stocks: Growth stocks are companies that are expanding rapidly. Instead of paying dividends to share-holders, they reinvest their earnings into the business to fuel further growth. These companies tend to have high stock prices because investors expect them to continue growing quickly. While growth stocks can deliver substantial returns, they are also vulnerable to market downturns if their growth slows down. Growth stocks teach your kids about betting on the future—these are companies with big ambitions, but they require time and patience to pay off.

4. Value Stocks: Value stocks are shares in companies that are considered undervalued by the market. These stocks may not be as exciting as growth stocks, but they offer a great opportunity to buy solid companies at a lower price. Value investing is about looking for bargains in the market—companies that are temporarily out of favor but still have strong fundamentals. Value stocks offer steady, reliable returns and teach your kids that patience is rewarded when the market eventually recognizes the true worth of these companies.

By investing in low-cost index funds that include a mix of large-cap, small-cap, growth, and value stocks, your kids will automatically diversify their investments across all four quadrants. This diversification reduces risk while still providing significant growth opportunities. Index funds also keep things simple, as they don't require them to constantly monitor or manage individual stock picks.

WHY IS REAL ESTATE A SIMPLE AND POWERFUL INVESTMENT?

Real estate is another important component of a balanced, long-term investment strategy. While stocks are great for growing wealth, real estate offers additional benefits that complement a stock portfolio, such as regular income and long-term appreciation. Here's why real estate is a simple yet powerful investment that your kids should consider:

It's Tangible: Real estate is something your kids can see and touch—a house, a piece of land or an apartment building. Unlike stocks, which can feel abstract, real estate is a physical asset that is easier to understand. Explain to your children that by owning real estate, they are investing in something tangible that has intrinsic value. Whether it's a home or rental property, they are building equity over time.

Generates Passive Income: One of the biggest advantages of real estate is the ability to generate passive income through rent. If they own rental property, they can earn money every month from tenants. This income can help pay off the mortgage, be reinvested or simply used for other expenses. Real estate provides a steady stream of cash flow that is separate from the stock market, offering a layer of financial stability.

Appreciation Over Time: Like stocks, real estate generally appreciates in value over the long term. While property values can fluctuate, the overall trend is upward, especially in desirable locations. Explain to your kids that owning real estate means holding onto an asset that grows in value, creating wealth as they pay off their mortgage and as property prices rise. Real estate rewards long-term thinking, much like stocks.

Leverage: One of the unique benefits of real estate is the ability to use leverage—borrowing money (through a mortgage) to buy property. This means they can own and control a large asset with a relatively small amount of money upfront. Over time, as the property appreciates, they benefit from the entire value of the asset, not just their initial investment. Leverage can significantly boost their returns, as long as they manage it wisely.

By investing in both stocks and real estate, your children will have a balanced portfolio that offers both growth and stability. Stocks provide the potential for rapid growth, while real estate offers steady income and long-term appreciation. Together, these two investments complement each other and reduce overall risk.

WHAT ARE THE THREE SIMPLE STEPS TO FINANCIAL FREEDOM?

The beauty of investing is that by following some simple steps, achieving financial freedom can become simple. Here's a straightforward plan your children can follow to build wealth over time:

1. Save Consistently: The foundation of financial success is saving. Teach your kids to live below their means and set aside a portion of their income for investing. By building the habit of saving, they'll always have money to invest. It's not about starting big; it's about starting early and staying consistent. Even small amounts grow significantly over time thanks to compound interest.

2. Invest in Both Stocks and Real Estate: Once they've

saved, the next step is to invest that money. Low-cost index funds make stock investing simple and effective, allowing your kids to benefit from the growth of the market without needing to pick individual stocks. Real estate provides a tangible, stable investment that generates income and appreciates over time. Together, these two assets provide a balanced approach that delivers both growth and stability.

3. Stay the Course: The final, and perhaps hardest, step is to be patient and stick with the plan. Explain to your kids that the market will go up and down, but reacting to short-term movements can hurt their long-term goals. Successful investing is not about timing the market but time in the market. By leaving their investments alone and allowing them to grow, they'll reap the benefits of compounding returns. Patience and discipline are the true keys to financial success.

WHY IS SIMPLICITY ULTIMATELY THE BEST STRATEGY?

One of the biggest challenges your kids will face as investors is navigating the constant noise from the media, market experts and even friends or family. Every day, there will be news about market movements, economic changes and the latest hot stock. Teach them that successful investing is not about chasing the latest trend or reacting to every piece of news. It's about sticking to a simple plan and ignoring the distractions.

By keeping their investments simple—saving regularly, diversifying across stocks and real estate, and staying the course—your kids will avoid the emotional traps that cause many investors to make mistakes. The path to financial success doesn't require complexity, it requires consistency and patience. Remind them that wealth is built slowly and steadily, not overnight.

In the end, the path to financial freedom is simple:

Stocks: By investing in low-cost index funds that cover large-cap, small-cap, growth, and value stocks, your kids will automatically diversify their portfolio without needing to worry about picking individual winners. Index funds are simple, tax-efficient, and allow them to benefit from the overall growth of the market.

Real Estate: Real estate offers a stable, tangible investment that provides both rental income and long-term appreciation. It's a simple yet powerful complement to stock investing, balancing the volatility of the stock market with steady, reliable returns.

Stick to the Plan: The most important part of investing is staying disciplined. Teach your kids that once they've set their plan in motion, the best thing they can do is leave it alone and let time do the heavy lifting. Markets will fluctuate, but by sticking to their simple strategy, they'll see their wealth grow steadily over the years.

By following this simple, balanced approach, your children will be well on their way to building lasting wealth and achieving financial freedom. It really is that simple—save, invest and stay patient. With time, this straightforward strategy will reward them far more than any complex, short-term trading strategy ever could.

KEY TAKEAWAYS

- Teach kids to earn money through work or entrepreneurship.
- Help your kids distinguish between needs and wants when spending.
- Introduce investment concepts using relatable examples and real-world businesses.
- Cultivate an abundance mindset through giving and sharing.

CHAPTER 17

ACCELERATE WEALTH THROUGH NEVER ENDING LEARNING

"Treat yourself like a business. Invest in yourself and make sure you're always growing."
—Unknown

LESSON: WEALTH IS A LONG-TERM GAME, BUT YOU CAN SPEED UP your returns in the short-term by being a perpetual learner.

Teach your kids the value of investing in themselves by embracing lifelong learning. The good news is learning is accessible to all of us and doesn't require an Ivy League education. Learning doesn't stop once you graduate from high school or college. Opportunities for learning abound throughout your life if you stay committed to growth.

You can achieve long-term gains by putting in the work. Being consistent may sound like a boring concept, but a lot of excitement can come through long-term investing. Consistency is key and moves kids away from the right now mentality and toward the tomorrow mentality.

WHAT ARE SOME WAYS TO MAKE LEARNING ABOUT INVESTING MORE FUN FOR KIDS?

Interactive games; whether board games , video games, or apps can get kids engaged with basic business, finance and asset management principle. Your child can build skills like decision-making, risk assessment and strategic thinking while playing a game. Here are a few ideas:

Cash Flow for Kids: This board game teaches cash flow management, as players make decisions about careers, buying assets like stocks and real estate and taking out loans.

The Stock Market Game: Kids get a virtual $100,000 to invest in real stocks for a five-year period. They learn research, trading strategies and diversification by managing a portfolio. The game is ideal for kids in Grades 4 through 12.

Monopoly: This classic game shows the fundamentals of real estate investing. In Monopoly, kids can purchase and upgrade properties to generate rental income. Monopoly introduces kids to many real estate fundamentals like acquiring properties, managing cash flows and growing investments over time through development.

Lemonade Tycoon: In this app, kids can run a virtual lemonade stand. They can learn how to manage their inventory, determine demands, perfect their lemonade recipe, set their prices and advertise. The goal is to have a profitable business that will survive the 90 days of summer.

SMG InvestQuest: In this game, kids get hypothetical money to pick stocks, bonds and mutual funds and are able track their portfolio over a simulated five-year period. This free, fun and informative investing experience emphasizes diversification and long-term investing.

GravyStack: This app is a banking platform for kids and teens. It includes a bank account with a physical and virtual debit card. Parents and kids agree on the percentage of every dollar that automatically gets split into their Save, Spend and Share Jars. Because kids earn every dollar and they can only spend what's in their Spend Jar, they can learn smart spending habits in a safe environment.

WHAT ARE SOME OTHER INSPIRING WAYS TO LEARN ABOUT INVESTING?

You can do other activities with your kids to learn more about investing to create a life of financial freedom. Here are some ideas:

Plan a Money Trip: You can create a money trip by doing an activity with your kid that is money or business related. Many big companies offer facility tours where you can see the operations first-hand. Some companies also allow guests at shareholder meetings. Don't be afraid to use your imagination. When my daughter was a high school sophomore, I signed her up to attend the International Women's Forum in San Francisco. She was able to spend the day with female business owners who shared how they had failed multiple times before achieving success. The experience fueled her curiosity about business and showed her some of the challenges.

Attend an Investing Conference: Check with local universities and financial institutions to see if they offer opportunities for kids to learn about finances. For example, DePaul University in Chicago offers "The Invest for Kids Summer Investment Challenge," a five-day college immersion program for high school students interested in finance careers. Students are able to experience what it's like to be a finance student living on campus.

Locate Financial Literacy Programs: Junior Achievement USA offers programs that focus on financial literacy, entrepreneurship and work readiness. You can find programs and material appropriate for elementary, middle or high school students. The Securities Industry and Financial Markets Association (SIFMA) offers financial literacy and investor education programs tailored for kids and teens. The American Library Association promotes free financial literacy programs for kids and teens as well.

Join an Investment Club for Students: Investing clubs allow kids to learn collaboratively about investing through researching stocks and managing a portfolio together. You could even start your own neighborhood investing group for parents and kids. Your club could be a purely educational one, where kids pick hypothetical stocks to track and use pretend money to invest. Alternatively, parents could pool money to make small (real) investments for the club. As a parent, you can open a custodial brokerage account for your child.

Do an Internet Search: Search for local programs, summer camps or events hosted by financial educators, investment firms and nonprofits in your area specifically geared toward youth investment education.

Buy an Investment Property: The process of buying a property is an excellent way for your kid to learn multiple strategies of investing. Have them research properties by looking at listings, touring properties, calculating potential rental income and evaluating neighborhoods and property conditions. Then, you'll work together to calculate expenses like mortgage, taxes, and maintenance as well as evaluate cash flow. After purchasing, involve them in tasks like collecting rent, paying bills, approving repairs and tracking income/expenses.

Listen to Investing and Entrepreneurship Podcasts: Search for age-appropriate podcasts for your kids. Besides podcasts, there are also investing YouTube channels, websites and apps focused on making investing relatable and accessible for younger audiences using storytelling, characters and gamification.

Read *The Wall Street Journal*: *The Wall Street Journal* newspaper has a dedicated investing and markets section that provides in-depth analysis of market trends, economic conditions and individual stocks/sectors. Their personal finance columnists provide tips related to investing, retirement planning, taxes and managing wealth. Pick one topic regularly to discuss with your kid.

All of the activities I've outlined in this chapter require commitment on both you and your kid's part. Out of that commitment will come a new kind of relationship with your child, and the knowledge that financial freedom is not only possible, but probable.

Remember, you don't need to do it alone. Like any part of raising a child, it takes a village. We'll explore what that village might look like in it in our next chapter, where we focus on finding the best money mentor for your child.

180

KEY TAKEAWAYS

- Use your imagination and take into consideration your child's interests when planning a money trip.
- Teaching your kids about money can be fun.
- Take the time to try different ways to teach your kids about money.
- Download the educational calendar at www.401kid.education.

CHAPTER 18
CHOOSE A MONEY MENTOR COACH

"A great coach has the ability to recognize and nurture an individual's untapped potential, inspiring them to surpass their own expectations and achieve greatness."
—Michael Jordan

LESSON: PARENTS PLAY A CRUCIAL ROLE AS THEIR CHILDREN'S primary money mentors, but it's also important to encourage kids to seek out and learn from diverse, reputable financial role models.

As a parent, you are your child's most important money mentor. Even if your parents didn't teach you about money, you can still help your kids build healthy financial habits.

As a mentor, you are sharing knowledge and offering guidance and support. You are also a coach. You are helping your kid achieve their goals while providing feedback and accountability.

Beyond yourself, encourage your kids to have other powerful role models who can guide and motivate them to create wealth and live the life they envision. These money mentors or coaches could be people your kids know personally or people they admire. Be sure they avoid fake rich social media influencers.

Money mentors possess substantial financial knowledge,

practical experience and a willingness to share that wisdom with others. These mentors or coaches often have achieved their own financial success. In addition to that, they should have certain characteristics.

WHAT ARE GOOD CHARACTERISTICS TO LOOK FOR IN MONEY MENTORS?

In my experience, money mentors have the same traits as good coaches. While each coach might have a different personality and approach, they share some of the following characteristics:

Authenticity and Relatability: Successful money influencers are genuine, relatable and down-to-earth. They share their personal stories and struggles, which helps them to connect deeply with their audience.

Confidence and Charisma: They exude confidence in their knowledge, which builds trust. Their engaging personalities draw people in.

Transparency and Vulnerability: They are open about their failures and mistakes, making them more relatable.

Consistency and Reliability: They consistently provide valuable content and follow through on promises, building credibility.

Passion and Enthusiasm: Their passion for financial education is contagious. They genuinely want to help others improve their financial situations.

Humility and Willingness to Learn: Despite their expertise, they remain humble and open to learning from others.

Engagement and Responsiveness: They actively engage with their audience, fostering a sense of community.

These traits help establish themselves as trusted authorities in their field.

HOW DO YOU STAY IN MONEY CONVERSATIONS WITH YOUR KIDS?

Keep introducing new money mentors to your kids and encourage them to search for age-appropriate mentors based on who they relate to. As their primary money mentor, coach your kids through the process.

Remind them that money is a measurement game, not a thing game. Those who chase money never have money, but those who chase impact and create value live in abundance.

WHO ARE SOME GOOD MONEY MENTORS TO FOLLOW? IS THERE A GOOD MONEY MENTOR FOR UNMOTIVATED COLLEGE STUDENTS?

Gary Vaynerchuk (commonly known as Gary Vee) is a respected entrepreneur who uses a no-nonsense approach to personally connect with people. His authenticity (with a bit, okay, a lot of profanity) and transparency have earned him trust and respect from his followers. He built his career and fame around his entrepreneurial journey growing his family's liquor store into a multi-million-dollar wine library and e-commerce operation.

Gary Vee's message of hard work, hustle and perseverance resonates with many —especially the younger generation. He encourages entrepreneurs to push themselves and take action toward achieving their goals early on. He is a popular college commencement speaker as he stresses the importance of investing in yourself, taking more risks and taking advantage of being young.

Gary Vee says, "Your biggest advantage is your youth. And too many kids don't take advantage of time. So, I would take advantage of your youth and flexibility. Try to taste everything, play with everything, and figure out what you might be good at and what you might like."

Vee refers to something called the "five-year window" where kids around age 22 enter some of the greatest years of their lives. In this window kids have a unique opportunity to not play it safe and instead take risks and try to maximize as much money as they can make.

Through his speeches, podcasts and social media platforms, Vee provides advice about financial discipline, investing in yourself, recognizing opportunities and monetizing your skills and passions.

To date, Vee has about 44 million followers and makes about $200 million annually through his investments. His venture capital firm (VaynerX) allows him to invest in—and mentor—emerging companies and founders looking to build profitable businesses.

One of Gary Vee's most popular sayings is, "Legacy is greater than currency." In other words, creating something meaningful and impactful that will outlast you is more valuable than just focusing on accumulating money.

WHAT'S A GOOD WAY TO DESCRIBE MENTORS TO KIDS?

Use a sports analogy. Every great athlete has a coach. An athletic coach teaches and guides players in their sport. Coaches watch carefully while their players practice and play. They give instructions and advice to help their players improve their abilities.

A good coach encourages players to do their best, learn from their mistakes and never give up. With a coach's leadership, athletes can reach their full potential.

Coaches are like mentors. I've hired coaches for both myself and my kids as their knowledge can make all the difference.

Just like in pursuing financial freedom, success doesn't happen instantly. It takes work and sacrifice to accomplish what you want.

As an athlete who competes in Ironman triathlon competitions, I know personally what it takes to achieve the finisher medal. You don't just do an Ironman. You see the environment and observe what it takes to come in first, come in last, and not make the cutoff. It's all about sheer grit and determination. And sometimes it's a huge disappointment.

Money management requires the same kind of tenacity, resilience, patience, perseverance and careful planning to achieve success. That's why you, and your kids, need a money mentor.

WHAT ARE SOME GOOD WAYS TO FIND REPUTABLE MENTORS?

Finding impactful mentors is an activity you and your kids can do together. Following mentors introduces unique opportunities for conversations between you and your child about their posts. Follow reputable financial mentors who are disciplined and focused on the long-term, avoiding the allure of instant gratification. For instance, Grant Cardone is an entrepreneur, author, speaker and investor known as "the real estate guy" who has a net worth of $600 million.

Cardone has 95% of his wealth invested in real estate. He notes that when real estate prices fluctuate and the value comes down, the income from real estate is always taking care of him. At age 30, he started investing in real estate and has never looked back.

Cardone is all about creating impact and making a difference, especially with young people. The Grant Cardone Foundation's mission is to provide mentoring and financial literacy education to adolescents in underserved and at-risk populations, especially if there is no father figure present. Cardone's vision is to live in a world where every kid is provided the tools and mentorship they need to be successful in all aspects of their lives.

WHO ARE SOME FEMALE ENTREPRENEURS CREATING IMPACT?

There are also many successful female entrepreneurs. For example, Oprah Winfrey's net worth is a whopping $3 billion. Oprah is entirely self-made, coming from poverty. She became a media mogul with *The Oprah Winfrey Show.*

Throughout her career, Oprah Winfrey has used her platform and resources to support education, women's empowerment, global humanitarian efforts and various other charitable causes. Winfrey is one of the most philanthropic celebrities in the world.

From her early days in television, Oprah was savvy about negotiating ownership stakes in her shows and productions, allowing her to build equity over time. Oprah's wealth-building strategies seem to focus on building equity ownership in her own brands, investing in real estate, taking strategic stakes in public companies and providing early-stage funding to promising startups while maintaining a diversified portfolio.

Her philanthropic work, though, has created the most impact. One of her many endeavors is The Oprah Winfrey Leadership Academy for Girls in South Africa, which provides educational opportunities for disadvantaged girls from low-income families. She donated $40 million to establish the school in 2007.

Another female powerhouse investor is Sheryl Sandberg who is best known for her executive roles at major tech companies like Google and Meta (formerly Facebook). After selling most of her stake in Meta, she made a lot of money.

As an active investor, Sandberg uses an investment strategy of buying undervalued stocks and companies that she believes have strong fundamentals and potential for growth. Like many successful investors, Sandberg takes a long-term view and doesn't focus on short-term stock movements.

Sandberg provides seed funding to select early-stage startup companies, often those founded by women or focused on issues she cares about like diversity and women's empowerment. Currently, Sandberg focuses on making an impact through philanthropy with her $2.1 billion net worth.

Sheryl Sandberg's career journey is a testament to the impact that mentorship can have on somebody's success. As an economics student at Harvard, Larry Summers—the Treasury Secretary under President Bill Clinton—took Sandburg under his wing. Mentorship makes a difference.

Here's another example. Although Rihanna is a chart-topping, high-profile entertainer, it's what she's done offstage that has made her the wealthiest female musician in the world. When she launched her beauty line, Fenty Beauty, in 2017, it was an immediate success. Using New York Fashion Week as a publicity springboard, Rihanna led Fenty to a reported $72 million in sales in the first month. *Time* named her products one of their "Top 25 Inventions" of 2017. Today, her net worth is $1.4 billion.

Rihanna's brand is known for its commitment to diversity, offering beauty products for a far wider range of skin tones than most brands. Rihanna has since expanded to luxury fashion and lingerie, offering an inclusive array of sizes and advertising her products with diverse models.

At just 18, Rihanna founded the Believe Foundation to help critically ill children. At age 24, she launched the nonprofit Clara Lionel Foundation, which supports and funds education and early response programs around the world. For her philanthropic efforts, she was honored with the President's Award at the 2020 NAACP Image Awards.

These examples can inspire your kids to think bigger, and to dream about what's possible if they work hard and stay focused. Having a mentor can help them put those dreams into action.

WHAT ARE SOME WAYS TO FIND AND ENGAGE WITH MENTORS?

Involve your kids in activities that introduce them to potential mentors, such as attending conferences, listening to podcasts and participating in money trips. Spending quality time together on these activities also strengthens your relationship and opens lines of communication about money.

At the core, creating a 401Kid is all about interacting with your kid and doing activities with them. As you participate in financially focused activities, you'll be creating a lifelong bond. As you and your kid listen to podcasts together or attend events, you'll enhance that bond.

Spending quality time together is how parents and children build a strong, loving relationship. When parents set aside special moments to give a child their undivided attention and affection, it helps that child feel safe, valued and loved unconditionally. These positive experiences create an emotional bond that assures the child they can trust and depend on their parents.

It also opens the lines of communication so kids feel comfortable sharing their thoughts, feelings and questions as they grow. Be vulnerable and real with your kids about your relationship with money and allow them to see you are not perfect.

As a parent, share successes, failures and what you learned along the way. Incorporate what you would change if you could go back, and tailor this all to the age of your child. Let them know you'll be exploring the topic of wealth creation together.

ANY FINAL WORDS ON GETTING MY KID EXCITED ABOUT BEING A 401KID?

Encourage your kids to look up to role models who have achieved sustainable success through hard work and ethical means. By doing so, you empower them to pursue financial freedom and live the life they envision.

In the next chapter, we'll recap what it takes to raise a successful 401Kid.

———

KEY TAKEAWAYS

- Mentors can be both personal connections and public figures.
- Find appropriate mentors to guide your child to financial freedom.
- Focus on chasing impact rather than money.
- Download the find your mentor worksheet at www.401kid.education.

CHAPTER 19
THE GIFT OF GIVING BACK

"No one has ever become poor by giving."
—Anne Frank

LESSON: GIVING BACK IS A POWERFUL FORCE THAT NOT ONLY HELPS others but also brings profound personal fulfillment and creates stronger communities. By shifting our focus from self-centered pursuits to service and generosity, we can cultivate positive change in the world around us.

When Bill Gates was a kid, his parents gave him a weekly allowance. He could spend it how he chose, but as the holiday season approached, his parents asked how much he was planning to give to the Salvation Army at Christmas. That was his first introduction to philanthropy. Their message was clear: if you're in a position to help somebody, you should do it.

Gates has followed through on this message. In 2010, he created something called the Giving Pledge with Melinda French Gates and Bill Gates. The Giving Pledge is an open invitation for billionaires to publicly commit to give the majority of their wealth to philanthropy either during their lifetimes or in their wills.

You don't have to be a billionaire to become a philanthropist.

Giving back is like planting seeds in a garden. Just as a gardener plants seeds to grow beautiful flowers and delicious fruits, when we give back to others, we help our communities grow stronger and more vibrant. Giving back means sharing our time, talents and resources to help those around us. It's an important way to show kindness, compassion and gratitude for what we have. This chapter will explain why giving back is essential and tell a story that illustrates its importance, one that is understandable to both kids and adults.

WHY DOES GIVING BACK MATTER SO MUCH?

Giving back matters for the following reasons:

Builds Stronger Communities: When people give back, they help build stronger communities. Whether it's volunteering at a local food bank, participating in neighborhood clean-ups or mentoring younger students, these actions create a sense of unity and cooperation.

Creates Opportunities: Giving back often provides opportunities for those who may not have access to certain resources. Donating books to a library or school supplies to children in need can open up new worlds of learning and imagination.

Spreads Happiness: Acts of kindness and generosity can bring immense joy and happiness to both the giver and the receiver. It creates a ripple effect, where one good deed can inspire many others.

Teaches Valuable Lessons: For kids, giving back teaches them important values like empathy, responsibility and gratitude. For adults, it reinforces these values and reminds them of the impact they can have on others.

HOW DO WE TEACH OUR KIDS ABOUT GIVING IN A WAY THAT MATTERS MOST TO THEM?

In life, we often encounter the notion that happiness stems from power, possessions and the admiration of others. This perspective creates a false sense of reality, particularly in a world that heavily emphasizes material success and social status. Convincing young people to see beyond this mindset can be challenging, especially when they are bombarded with messages that equate worth with wealth and recognition.

I recall a compelling insight from Joe Polish, who, in his work with Genius Network, boldly stated that he disagrees with the idea that money doesn't buy happiness. He argues that those who believe this simply haven't given enough away. This statement encapsulates a paradox inherent in the act of giving, one that challenges conventional wisdom. The Giving Pledge, a commitment by wealthy individuals to give away a significant portion of their wealth, illustrates that the outcomes of generosity often defy our expectations.

It is crucial to instill in today's youth an understanding that there is a universal law: you cannot continuously draw from the stream of life without giving back. If you take without contributing, you deplete the stream's resources, ultimately leading to a dead-end journey for our children. This notion invites a profound discussion about the cyclical nature of life, where giving and receiving are intricately linked.

When we encourage giving, we are, in essence, building a vital foundation that replenishes the stream of life for others. The satisfaction derived from acts of kindness and generosity is profound. This energy stems from the realization that we operate from a place of abundance, that we have enough to share. When individuals refrain from giving, it often comes from a scarcity mentality—a belief that there is not enough to go around. This mindset breeds a lack of gratitude, making it difficult for people to appreciate what they have.

The Giving Pledge fosters an attitude of abundance, promoting the belief that "I have enough, and I want to help others have some too." This mindset cultivates an environment ripe for ideas, innovation and collaboration. It encourages creativity and the sharing of resources, leading to greater collective achievements. In contrast, a scarcity mentality often leads to isolation, fear, and a protective stance, resulting in a lack of community and support.

I admire Elon Musk's perspective on competition and collaboration in the tech industry. In a field often characterized by cutthroat competition, he challenges the conventional wisdom that suggests one must protect their ideas at all costs. Musk advocates for sharing and encouraging others to build upon those ideas. This approach aligns perfectly with the spirit of the Giving Pledge, emphasizing that innovation thrives in an environment where collaboration is prioritized over competition.

When we teach our children the importance of giving, we instill in them a core value of service. This foundational principle enriches their lives, guiding them to understand that a life dedicated to helping others is invariably more fulfilling and joyful than one focused solely on self-interest. We all know people who constantly ask, "What's in it for me?" They tend to drain the energy of those around them, creating an atmosphere of negativity. In contrast, those who focus on others understand that by giving, they ultimately win—both in terms of personal satisfaction and the positive impact they have on their communities.

The spirit of giving transforms lives. This principle is evident in various contexts, including religious teachings and support programs like the 12-step recovery movement. The cycle of addiction often stems from self-obsession, where individuals feel they can never have enough. This relentless pursuit leads them to violate their values, harm others and plunge deeper into their struggles.

The solution lies in a profound shift—from a self-centered existence to a life centered around service to others. While this idea may seem counterintuitive to the logical mind, it is truly the path to freedom. As articulated in many spiritual teachings, the plea is often, "Relieve me of the bondage of self so that I may better do Thy will." What is that will? Service to others.

This fundamental principle is deeply rooted in the teachings of various religious doctrines and is a cornerstone of recovery programs. The concept of selflessness is emphasized in many spiritual traditions, teaching that true happiness comes from serving others and contributing to the greater good. Similarly, 12-step programs often highlight the importance of helping others as a means of recovery, reinforcing the idea that a focus on the self can lead to destructive patterns.

Teaching kids the flywheel of giving not only provides them with the tools to live a happier life but also cultivates a generation committed to serving others. By instilling a sense of gratitude and the understanding that their actions can positively affect the world around them, we empower our kids to create a ripple effect of kindness and generosity.

Moreover, instilling the spirit of giving can lead to long-term benefits for both individuals and communities. Children who learn to give back often grow into adults who prioritize social responsibility and community engagement. They are more likely to volunteer, support charitable causes and advocate for social justice, contributing to a more compassionate, equitable society.

Teaching kids about the flywheel of giving is an invaluable investment in their future and the future of our communities. It challenges the prevailing narrative of self-interest, offering a more profound understanding of happiness and fulfillment. By nurturing a spirit of generosity, we not only enrich their lives but also create a more interconnected and thriving world. This journey of giving, rooted in abundance and service, will ultimately lead to a brighter future for all.

ANY OTHER INSPIRING STORIES TO HELP BRING THE POINT HOME?

I'll never forget the story of Dave Tatge, sitting in his parking lot as he shared insights about his company. It was just a few months after my business had imploded, and we were discussing the success of his enterprise compared to the failure of mine. I asked him about the real estate he owned and the achievements that led him to build such a thriving organization.

As our conversation shifted to the building we were standing in front of, Dave surprised me by saying, "Well, I don't own that building." He pointed to the structure across the street and added, "My operations manager owns that building." Then he gestured to another building down the street and continued, "And that one too. I actually put those in a pool for my employees who work at that facility—they own that building."

At that moment, I looked at him in disbelief and asked, "Dave, what do you want?" He simply replied, "I don't want a lot." He explained that over the years, he had discovered a profound truth: when you make your employees owners, you can't spend the money fast enough.

It was then that I experienced a significant epiphany about the contrast between my mindset and his. Dave exemplified the spirit of giving and service to others on a completely different level. He included everyone in his mission—his employees, vendors and everyone else associated with the business. He emphasized that we must do better and ensure that everyone shares in the profits. He never cut corners, it was always about striving for excellence and rewarding everyone involved. As a result, everyone pulled in the same direction, and he virtually had no competition.

Reflecting on my own experience, I realized that I had built my business on a model that could only be described as a dictatorship. It was self-centered, focused on my success, rather than valuing the collective wisdom of others. At the time, I didn't see it, but looking back on that implosion, I can see how self-centeredness permeated every decision I made. l. If your organization is filled with individuals who feel undervalued, you simply won't make much progress. In contrast, if you cultivate partnerships and foster collaboration, you will become an unstoppable force.

This is why the Giving Pledge is so powerful and profound— it shifts the focus from individual success to collective achievement. As our children embark on their own journeys in life, whether in marriage, business or on a sports team, it's essential that they understand the importance of collaboration and shared goals.

Consider the parent who angrily confronts a soccer coach because their child isn't getting enough playing time. What message does that send to the child? It implies that their individual needs are more important than the team's success. This mindset can be detrimental, as it fosters a sense of entitlement rather than teamwork and cooperation.

In teaching kids the value of collective effort and the spirit of giving, we empower them to understand that true fulfillment comes from contributing to something greater than themselves. By instilling these principles, we prepare them to navigate life with a mindset that prioritizes collaboration, service and community, ultimately leading to a more harmonious and successful existence for all.

Dave Tatge's story is a profound reminder of the impact that leadership and organizational culture can have on both individual fulfillment and collective success. By prioritizing employee ownership, fostering collaboration and embracing a mindset of abundance, we can create environments that not only thrive but also cultivate a sense of purpose and community. These principles are not just applicable in business settings; they resonate in all aspects of life, encouraging us to work together for the common good and to raise future generations with values that emphasize service, collaboration and generosity.

ARE THERE ANY OTHER STORIES TO USE AS EXAMPLES ABOUT THE IMPORTANCE OF GIVING BACK?

A great, kid-friendly story about giving back is the tale of Maya and the Magic Garden. Once upon a time, in a small village nestled between rolling hills and a sparkling river, there lived a little girl named Maya. Maya was known for her bright smile and her love for gardening. She spent her days tending to her family's garden, which was filled with colorful flowers, juicy fruits and fresh vegetables.

One summer, a severe drought hit the village. The rivers dried up, and the gardens withered. The villagers were worried as their crops failed, and food became scarce. Maya's garden, which had always been lush and green, began to turn brown and brittle.

One morning, as Maya walked through the village, she noticed a group of children looking sad and hungry. She remembered the joy her garden had brought to her and decided she wanted to help. Maya ran back home and gathered all the seeds she had saved over the years. She filled a basket with the seeds and started visiting each house in the village, sharing her precious seeds with her neighbors.

"These seeds are special," she told them. "They need a lot of love and care, but they will grow into the most beautiful plants and give us food to eat."

The villagers were touched by Maya's generosity. They planted the seeds and, with Maya's help and guidance, started caring for their new gardens. Maya showed them how to water the plants sparingly and use mulch to keep the soil moist.

Weeks passed, and slowly, the seeds began to sprout. Green shoots peeked through the dry soil, and soon, vibrant flowers and healthy vegetables started to grow. The village, once dry and desolate, was now bursting with life and color.

Maya's act of giving back had transformed her village. The

villagers, inspired by her kindness, began to help each other more. They shared their harvests, taught each other new skills and worked together to ensure everyone had enough to eat.

The village thrived, and the sense of community grew stronger. Maya's small act of giving back had created a ripple effect of generosity and cooperation. She learned that even the smallest acts of kindness could make a big difference in the lives of others.

HOW DID YOU GET YOUR PERSPECTIVE TO CHANGE?

A great influence in my life has been participating in Ironman competitions. Widely considered to be one of the most physically challenging endurance contests, in a single day, you complete a 2.4-mile swim, a 112-mile bike ride and a 26.2-mile run. I completed my first Ironman in Arizona in 2017. It was exhilarating, but my most profound Ironman experience was when I teamed up with a young man with cerebral palsy, Patrick Utitus-Canez. Although he could not walk, he had completed over 30 marathons and had always wanted to be an Ironman.

For an athlete like Patrick to compete in an Ironman, someone would have to tow him in a raft during the swim, push or pull him with the bike during cycling, and push him in a jogger for the run. I was honored when the founder of 2Gether We Live, an organization that seeks to make a positive difference for those with disabilities or illness, asked me to help Patrick achieve his goal.

This involved not just grueling training for about a year but also bankrolling and designing a new bike that would allow Patrick to ride in the front (rather than being pulled behind it). I threw myself into a fundraising campaign. Unlike things I had wanted in my past, this was not about buying something new to feed my desires. Instead, it was about helping someone else achieve more in life—about the impact that my money could make.

The race itself was a revelatory experience. I barely made it through the whole thing, but the feeling of accomplishment on the other side was unlike anything I'd ever experienced. When Patrick and I reached the beach after the swim portion, the crowds went absolutely nuts. I was overwhelmed.

We had the honor of inspiring many strangers, a feeling that still lifts my heart years later. This experience brought me a deep sense of personal fulfillment that I'd never felt before. All the endorphin rushes I experienced during my business wheeling and dealing didn't even come close.

Throughout my life, I pursued what others told me was important: money, status and prestige. While I studiously accumulated more *things*, none of them ever brought me peace.

Before my Ironman experience with Patrick, everything was about me and what I got or didn't get. I was an army of one. The experience with Patrick gave me a different perception: the power of we. As a result, I developed more personal friendships and connections than any business deal ever brought me, fueling my ability and desire to make an impact.

In a way, giving back is also like tending a garden, much like investing is. With care and generosity, we can help our communities grow and flourish. Whether through small acts of kindness or larger efforts, every contribution matters. Let's all plant the seeds of giving and watch our world become a more beautiful and compassionate place.

TEACHING CHILDREN THE POWER OF SERVICE AND MAKING THINGS BETTER

The most fundamental lesson we can give to our children is the importance of service. Service shapes who we are and how we show up in the world. Being of service to their friends, family, classmates and community is key to developing their character. But why is this so important?

Service to others leads to gratitude and personal growth. The more we serve, the more value we create and the greater the rewards we receive. However, money is merely a byproduct of what we do—it is not the ultimate goal. Every spiritual teacher across time has emphasized that true happiness and fulfillment come from service. It's a result of contributing meaningfully to others.

When this principle becomes part of their DNA, children wake up each day asking, "How can I help? This mindset changes how they operate in the world, making them more grateful, fulfilled and ultimately happier.

While this book focuses on teaching kids about money, financial success is actually the final step. Money is the natural outcome of a life rooted in service, value and meaningful contributions. The real goal is to raise happy, productive and grateful human beings. When people are content, humble and open to learning, they naturally create more value. With that mindset, financial success becomes easier, but it is never the main focus.

Consider the example of Mark Zuckerberg with Facebook. He didn't wake up one day and decide to become a billionaire by the time he was 20. Instead, he asked, "How can I create something that connects people and fosters friendships?" His focus was on building something better, improving the way people interacted and serving his community at Harvard. His success came from an attitude of contribution and service, not from a desire to chase money.

Similarly, Jeff Bezos with Amazon didn't start out with the goal of building a billion-dollar company. He focused on how to be of maximum service to his customers. In countless interviews, he emphasizes his commitment to providing the best experience —faster, cheaper and better for the customer. At the heart of his philosophy is service, and the extraordinary success of Amazon is a natural result of that commitment to serving others.

This book isn't just about teaching kids to manage money. It's about teaching them the principles of service, values and gratitude—the foundations of a fulfilling and successful life. Money is simply a byproduct of living by these values.

———

KEY TAKEAWAYS

- Giving back is like tending a garden. If you don't tend your garden, you won't reap the bountiful harvest.
- Giving back teaches important values like empathy, responsibility, and gratitude.
- Giving back is a way to create value in our world.
- Download the Giving Workbook at www.401kid.education.

CHAPTER 20
THE "WE" JOURNEY

"I am not afraid of storms, for I am learning how to sail my ship."
—Louisa May Alcott

LESSON: EASY CHILDHOOD, HARD LIFE; HARD CHILDHOOD, EASY LIFE.

Teaching your kids about money is not just a task—it's a journey, and one that is as much about your own growth as it is about theirs. It's a process that will shape both of you, filled with lessons learned, mistakes made and opportunities to bond deeply as you navigate the complexities of financial literacy together. The journey is not about perfection or reaching a specific destination. It's about equipping your kids with the tools and mindset to thrive in a world that will undoubtedly throw challenges their way.

WHAT IS A PARENT'S ROLE IN THE "WE" JOURNEY?

As parents, we often think our role is to guide and teach. What we sometimes forget is that teaching our kids about money is a learning experience for us too. It's an opportunity to be vulnerable and authentic, to share our own successes and failures, and to demonstrate that it's okay to make mistakes. This process allows us to model resilience, persistence, and the importance of continuous learning. In doing so, we provide our children with a powerful blueprint for their own financial journey.

When you openly discuss the financial lessons you've learned —whether it's the importance of saving, how you overcame debt, or even where you stumbled along the way—you're showing your children that learning about money isn't a linear path. It's filled with ups and downs. More importantly, you're teaching them that mistakes are part of the journey, not something to be feared.

COULD THIS HELP FORM A BETTER BOND WITH MY CHILD?

Few things in life create a bond like walking side by side with your child as they learn something new. When you talk to your kids about money, it's an opportunity to connect on a deeper level. You get to show them who you are not just as a parent, but as a human being who has experienced life's victories and setbacks.

This kind of openness fosters trust and creates a safe space for your kids to share their own fears and questions about money. They will feel more comfortable talking about their successes and struggles if they see that you're willing to do the same. Financial literacy becomes not just a set of skills to learn, but a shared family value that brings you closer.

One of the greatest gifts you can give your children is the ability to navigate life's inevitable hardships. Don't shield them from the bumps and bruises along the way. Let them experience the consequences of their choices, whether it's running out of their allowance because they spent too much or missing out on a purchase because they didn't save enough.

Encourage your children to see setbacks as learning opportunities. When they fall, don't rush to protect them—be there as a guide, a coach and a cheerleader. Show them how to dust themselves off and try again. This will instill resilience and a mindset that will serve them well beyond their financial life.

In teaching your children about money, emphasize the power of a positive mindset. While it's important to acknowledge challenges, it's equally important to focus on possibilities. Encourage them to think about what's possible, rather than what's out of reach. Frame financial learning as a series of opportunities rather than obstacles.

If there's something you don't know, don't be afraid to admit it. Teach your children the value of seeking out experts, asking questions and learning from those who have more experience. Whether it's reading books, attending seminars, or simply asking someone for advice, this mindset will help both you and your children continuously grow.

ISN'T THIS REALLY ALL ABOUT THE MONEY?

At the end of the day, teaching your kids about money isn't really about the money. It's about the journey of helping them build a life filled with purpose, meaning and financial security. It's about guiding them to become thoughtful, responsible individuals who can contribute value to the world around them. It's also about setting them up for a future where they can make informed decisions, avoid the pitfalls you may have encountered and create opportunities not just for themselves but for future generations.

WHAT ARE THE REWARDS OF WATCHING MY KID GROW?

Perhaps the most rewarding part of this journey is watching your children mature and flourish. There's nothing more fulfilling than seeing them apply the lessons you've taught them and develop into financially responsible adults who are capable of handling life's ups and downs with confidence. This transformation won't happen overnight, and there will be plenty of missteps along the way, but every step forward is a victory.

As their parent, you are their guide, their coach and their biggest cheerleader. Your role is to encourage them when they fall, remind them of the value of perseverance, and celebrate their successes, no matter how small.

This book is the culmination of a lifelong passion for helping families like yours navigate the world of money with intention, grace and a sense of possibility. I'm with you on this journey— because it's a journey I've walked myself, with my own children, through successes and setbacks. I hope that the lessons shared here inspire you to embark on this journey with your kids, knowing that the rewards will last a lifetime and beyond. Together, we can create a future where financial literacy is not a mystery but a shared, empowering experience that transforms not only our children but also ourselves.

Remember, this book isn't a comprehensive guide or a "catch-all." It's the beginning. Take a moment to sit down with your kids. Start a conversation, and begin a journey together. As you embark on this path, both you and your children will learn more. Along the way, new opportunities and teachers will naturally appear. I once heard someone say that as you start a journey and build momentum, your vision broadens. You won't have all the answers right away—answers come with the process itself.

The two main objectives of this book are simple: start the conversation now, and make this a bonding activity with your child. I'd love to hear how it's going, so feel free to drop me a note at walter@familycfo.net or visit www.401kid.org.

KEY TAKEAWAYS

- Kids are bound to face adversity throughout their lives so you want to teach them to be resilient early on so they can handle these challenges.
- You aren't doing your kids any favors by overprotecting them.
- Teach your kids to be gritty and do hard things so they can become resilient and create value in the world.
- Take action today to ensure that your kid becomes a 401Kid.
- Give your kid the gift of financial freedom.
- It's never too early to start.

ENDNOTES

INTRODUCTION

1. https://www.cnbc.com/2013/11/22/buffett-how-to-teach-your-kids-about-moneycommentary.html

1. WHEN AND HOW TO TALK TO YOUR KIDS ABOUT MONEY (NOW)

1. *13 Financial Literacy Games for children and adults (gamification resources).* Fitzsimons Credit Union. (2021, August 5). https://www.fitzsimonscu.com/financial-literacy-games-for-children-and-adults/.

4. THE POWER OF EARLY HABITS—WHY IT'S CRUCIAL TO INSTILL POSITIVE HABITS IN YOUR KIDS

1. Fogg, BJ. *Tiny Habits: The Small Changes That Change Everything.* 2021. Eugene, OR: Harvest House Publishers.

6. BEYOND SPENDING: EXPLAINING MONEY'S MULTIPLE ROLES TO KIDS

1. CBS News. Giannis Antetokounmpo and Calamos Investments Partner Up on Sustainable Investment Fund. March 31, 2023. https://www.cbsnews.com/video/giannis-antetokounmpo-and-calamos-investments-partner-up-on-sustainable-investment-fund/.

8. FOMO AND ENVY ARE TODAY'S CANCER

1. American Psychological Association. (n.d.). *Apa PsycNet.* American Psychological Association. https://psycnet.apa.org/record/2008-10897-005.
2. Altuwairiqi, M., Jiang, N., & Ali, R. (2019, June 17). *Problematic attachment to social media: Five behavioural archetypes.* MDPI. https://www.mdpi.com/1660-4601/16/12/2136.

9. TAKE RISKS: RAISE KIDS THAT AREN'T AFRAID TO TRY

1. Döpfner, M. Jeff Bezos interview with Axel Springer CEO on Amazon, Blue Origin, family. (2018, April 28). Business Insider. https://www.businessin sider.com/jeff-bezos-interview-axel-springer-ceo-amazon-trump-blue-origin-family-regulation-washington-post-2018-4.

10. THINK LIKE AN OWNER

1. *Rethinking fear of failure*. GEM Global Entrepreneurship Monitor. (n.d.). https://www.gemconsortium.org/news/rethinking-fear-of-failure.

11. CREATE EXCESS WITH YOUR KIDS

1. Centers for Disease Control and Prevention. (2024, August 5). *Suicide - health, United States*. Centers for Disease Control and Prevention. https://www.cdc.gov/nchs/hus/topics/suicide.htm#:.

2. Lima-Strong, C., Zakrzewski, C., Oremus, W. & Nix, N. (2024, Jan. 31). Meta's Zuckerberg apologies to child abuse victims in emotional Senate hearing. *The Washington Post*. https://www.washingtonpost.com/technol ogy/2024/01/31/senate-hearing-child-safety-tech-ceos-zuckerberg/.

ABOUT THE AUTHOR

Walter Clarke is a financial expert and educator dedicated to helping families successfully navigate their finances. After working in investment management for 20 years, he founded Family CFO to help wealthy families achieve financial longevity and improved family dynamics. Clarke has also been an adjunct financial educator at more than 10 universities, including the University of California, Berkeley; the University of California, Los Angeles; and the Tecnologico de Monterrey, for over two decades. Through parenting three children, and learning many lessons along the way, Clarke is committed to helping other parents teach their kids how to create value and impact—and secure their financial future in the process. *401Kid* is his second book.

Connect with Walter at walter@familycfo.net. To learn more, go to www.401kid.education and www.magicpenny.education.

ABOUT THE PUBLISHER

Legacy Launch Pad is a boutique publishing company that works with entrepreneurs from all over the world. For more information about Legacy Launch Pad Publishing, go to:

www.legacylaunchpadpub.com